Luke comes alive!

Luke comes alive!

John Blanchard

 EVANGELICAL PRESS

EVANGELICAL PRESS
16/18 High Street,
Welwyn, Hertfordshire, AL6 9EQ,
England.

© Evangelical Press 1986

First published 1977
Second edition 1986

This book was formerly published under the title
Look through Luke

Scripture references are taken from the
New International Version,
Hodder & Stoughton, 1979.

BL British Library Cataloguing in Publication Data
Blanchard, John, *1932-*
 Luke comes alive!: guidelines for personal
Bible reading. —— 2nd ed.
 1. Bible. N.T. Luke —— Devotional
literature
 I. Title II. Blanchard, John, *1932-*
Look through Luke
242'.2   BS2593

 ISBN 0-85234-223-3

Typeset by Computerset, Harmondsworth, Middx.
Printed in Great Britain by Cox & Wyman, Reading.

Introduction

Some years ago I wrote a book called *Read Mark Learn*, a series of Bible reading notes for people beginning the Christian life. It covered the Gospel of Mark in forty-five daily readings, and was written because I was convinced that, in spite of the existence of a number of Bible reading 'systems', there was a specific need for a book deliberately written with the new Christian in mind.

To my great surprise, I discovered that the book was not only being used to help those beginning the Christian life, but by many who had been Christians for years. In addition, it was being used in group activities such as house meetings, youth camps, church Bible studies and the like — to say nothing of its use by hard-pressed preachers in search of sermon outlines!

As a result, not only has *Read Mark Learn* now run to sixteen editions in twenty years, but there has been an increasing demand for another book to succeed it, and specifically for a book on another of the Gospels. This outside pressure has coincided with a deepening conviction of my own that many Christians have no regular guidelines for their personal Bible reading, or are dissatisfied with the system they are using. The outcome of these pressures was *Look Through Luke*, first published in 1977. *Luke Comes Alive!* is a major revision of that work.

The format of the book will already be obvious, but there are a few points that I would like to make by way of specific introduction.

Firstly, the notes are about twice the length of those in *Read Mark Learn*, and this is quite deliberate. My guess is that as far as personal daily Bible reading is concerned a disturbing number of Christians are making do with what we could call 'a look and a promise'. My earnest hope is that *Luke Comes Alive!* will help many of them to move away from this hit-and-miss business to a much more sustained approach. As a very rough guideline, my hope would be that a Christian using these notes would be prepared to take twenty to thirty minutes in carefully following through the reading and notes set out for each day.

Secondly, I have deliberately refrained from using quotations or illustrations from any other source except the Bible itself. There would have been nothing wrong in doing so, of course, but in preparing these studies my great concern has been to let the Bible speak for itself. It is always exhilarating to see how wonderfully God's Word fits together, and I hope that those using these notes will share in that experience.

Thirdly, a word about translations. We live at a time when we are being deluged with new translations and paraphrases of the Bible, and any preacher or writer on biblical themes has to come to terms with the situation. In preparing these notes I have based my studies on the *New International Version*, which is arguably the most helpful translation currently available in the English language. It would therefore be ideal if you followed the NIV text when using *Luke Comes Alive!* but this is by no means essential.

As with *Read Mark Learn*, these notes may prove helpful in group activities, but they have been written with the individual reader primarily in mind. That being so, let me repeat the suggestions I made in the introduction to *Read Mark Learn* as to how they should be best used:

1. As you come to the Bible each day, take time to pray that God will help you to understand what you are about to read.

2. Read slowly and carefully the passage indicated at the top of the section.

3. Read the notes for the day, looking back to the passage in Luke whenever a particular verse or phrase is quoted, and looking up every other Bible reference as it is mentioned.

4. Look up the text quoted at the foot of the section and think how it fits in with the day's reading.

5. Keep a notebook handy and jot down anything you think is especially helpful or relevant to your own life.

6. Pray that God will help you to live out the implications of whatever particular truths he has impressed upon you during your time of study and meditation.

The Gospel of Luke is a very exciting book, not least because it points its readers clearly and constantly to the Lord Jesus Christ as man's all-sufficient Saviour. My prayer is that these notes will help many people to follow Luke's directions.

JOHN BLANCHARD
Banstead,
Surrey.
April 1986

1

God speaking

Luke 1:1-17

When reading and studying the Bible, nothing is more important than to realize that it is *God's Word*, not merely a collection of religious ideas put together by good men. The authority of the Bible comes not from the calibre of its human authors, but from the character of its divine Author, the living and eternal God. In today's opening reading in Luke's Gospel this comes across in two ways.

The word that comes from God
It is always interesting to notice the immediate purpose for which certain parts of the Bible were written (two clear examples of this are John 20:30,31 and 1 John 5:13). In the passage before us we discover that Luke wrote his book to a man called Theophilus, who may have been an important official, judging by the way Luke addressed him (v.3), and the purpose of his writing was to confirm in the mind of Theophilus the things he had already been told (v.4). But how did Luke know these things?

First of all, he knew them by *revelation*; he speaks of 'the things that have been fulfilled among us' (v.1). Christianity is not based on ideas, but on events, and in those events God fulfilled promises he had already given. Then Luke knew these things by *confirmation*; he says that the facts 'were handed down to us by those who from the

first were eyewitnesses' (v.2) of what God had said and
done (compare 1 John 1:1-3 and 2 Peter 1:16-18).
Finally, Luke knew these things by *investigation*; he says,
'I myself have carefully investigated everything from the
beginning' (v.3). Now Luke was a doctor (see Colossians
4:14), a man used to making close examinations and
unlikely to lend his name to vague theories and
superstitions. As you study his book you will discover
that Luke is a stickler for *facts* and *details*. That is
precisely why he set out to write 'an orderly account'
(v.3) of the events that had shaken the world.

The word that came through Gabriel

Luke begins his account with an unlikely couple, an
elderly priest called Zechariah and his wife Elizabeth.
They were godly in life (v.6), but to their great sorrow
they were childless (v.7). When Zechariah was on duty
in the temple one day, an angel suddenly appeared to
him (vv.8-11). Not surprisingly the old man was 'gripped
with fear' (v.12), but the angel told him the great news
that Elizabeth was to have a son (v.13). Notice that this
was specifically said to be in answer to prayer. Notice,
too, that Zechariah was given one clear instruction —
the child was to be called John (v.13). Then came a
series of amazing prophecies about this unborn child. He
would be a cause of great delight to many people (v.14),
he would be counted great even in God's eyes (v.15), he
would exercise great personal discipline (v.15) and be
filled with the Holy Spirit from his birth (v.15). His life's
work would be similar to that of the great prophet Elijah,
calling people to repentance, and as a result many
disobedient Jews would turn back to God (vv.16,17).

This prophecy was fulfilled to the letter (see Matthew
3:1-3) because, as we shall see more fully in our next
study, the word that came through Gabriel was a word
that came from God. God still speaks today, through
creation, world events, the lives of Christians and in

many other ways; but he speaks most clearly through
his infallible, unchanging Word, the Bible (see Psalm
19:7-9).

As you close this first study thank God for his infallible
Word, the Bible, and submit yourself afresh to its divine
authority over every part of your life.

'All Scripture is God-breathed' (2 Timothy 3:16).

2

Man responding

Luke 1:18-25

The angel's prophecy had been astonishing — surely too
good to be true? With simple honesty, Luke now records
the reaction of Zechariah and Elizabeth. Three words
will help us to sum these up.

Doubtful

Zechariah surely *wanted* to believe his ears, but he had
one major difficulty — surely both he and Elizabeth were
too old to have a child? (v.18) His response was natural,
but he had missed the point that the message was
supernatural. The angel answered, 'I am Gabriel. I
stand in the presence of God' (v.19). The angel's
message came from heaven, not from hospital! Zechariah's unbelief was made more serious by the fact that he
was refusing to accept that God had answered prayer.
There is another illustration of this in Acts 12 — see
especially verses 5 and 12-16. The God we worship is the

God of the impossible, who is 'able to do immeasurably more than all we ask or imagine, according to his power that is at work within us' (Ephesians 3:20). We dare not limit him in our asking, nor in his answering.

Dumb

Gabriel's response (a reflection of God's) to Zechariah's unbelief was sudden and severe. He was to be struck dumb as a direct result of his unbelief and would not regain his voice until the promised child had been born (v.20). What a vivid lesson about the importance of taking God at his word! There are other New Testament illustrations of this: Matthew 13:58 and Mark 6:5,6, for instance. God has inserted the principle of *faith* into his dealings with men and none of the blessings of the gospel are possible without it: 'Without faith it is impossible to please God, because anyone who comes to him must believe that he exists and that he rewards those who earnestly seek him' (Hebrews 11:6). If only we knew how much blessing we missed, or how much loss we suffered, because of our downright unbelief, we would surely be ashamed!

Delighted

The spotlight now switches to Elizabeth who, some time later, discovered that she was expecting a baby (v.24). It is interesting how Elizabeth's reaction differed from that of her husband. Her immediate response was 'The Lord has done this for me' (v.25). There is no suggestion here that this was to be a virgin birth; it is clear that Zechariah was the father of the child. The remarkable thing about it was that God had graciously given Elizabeth special enabling to conceive, carry and give birth to the child at an advanced age. But Elizabeth went on to say that the Lord had done something else: 'He has shown his favour and taken away my disgrace among the people' (v.25). To the Jews, childlessness was not merely sad; it was significant. It was a sign of God's disfavour. A man could even divorce his wife if she did not bear him children! Because of this Elizabeth had spent years in disgrace, with people mocking her barrenness and inferring that this was a judgement on her sin. There is another example of this kind of heartless thinking in John 9:1,2. It is certainly true that all affliction can be traced back to the original sin of Adam; it is true that the sins of the parents are sometimes visited on their children; it is also true that one's own sins can be a direct cause of suffering; but it is *not* true that every affliction is the direct result of a particular sin. Pain and suffering are not necessarily signs of God's anger; Proverbs 3:11,12 and Revelation 3:19 tell us that the exact opposite is sometimes the case. For Elizabeth, only one thing mattered; she had found favour with God. No Christian could have a greater concern than that! (See 1 Thessalonians 4:1.)

'A good man obtains favour from the Lord' (Proverbs 12:2).

3

God's mysterious ways

Luke 1:26-38

In today's reading, Luke continues to establish the background to everything else that he is to write. So far, the action has taken place in Jerusalem and an unnamed town in Judea. Now we move on six months and the scene switches to a town called Nazareth in Galilee. Here

we find a young woman called Mary, a relative of
Elizabeth (v.36), who was 'pledged to be married to a
man named Joseph' (v.27). The action can now be
captured in four paragraphs.

A message is announced
Again, the angel Gabriel was the messenger (v.26) and
his message to Mary was truly amazing. Firstly, he told
her that in a very special way she had 'found favour with
God' (v.30). On hearing this, Mary was speechless,
unable to grasp what this meant (v.29). Notice carefully
that she was startled not so much by the angel's
appearance, but by his *words*. She was stunned to think
that she had found favour with God — a lovely lesson in
humility. But the heart of the angel's message was even
more startling: like Elizabeth, she was to give birth to a
son, in this case to be called Jesus (v.31). We shall return
to the rest of the angel's message later.

A miracle is assumed
Mary's first words to the angel were 'How will this be,
since I am a virgin?' (v.34) Whereas Zechariah did not
believe the angel, Mary *did* believe him, but was
naturally puzzled as to how such a thing could be
achieved. It is a sin to doubt that God will do what he
says, but not to admit ignorance of how he will do it. The
angel's answer to Mary's question was breathtaking
(v.35). There was to be a biological miracle, resulting in
what we now call the virgin birth. The *power* by which
God did this was the power of the Holy Spirit; the
principle under which he did it is that 'Nothing is
impossible with God' (v.37).

The Messiah is anticipated
The Old Testament is full of prophecies about God
sending the Messiah (which means the Anointed One).
Amazingly, the first veiled prophecy was made to the

devil! (See Genesis 3:15.) Notice that the one who would eventually conquer the devil would be the seed of the *woman* (whereas one normally speaks of the seed of a man). From then on, one detail after another was added until we come towards the last of the prophecies before the Messiah came (vv.32,33,35). Notice particularly that the child was to be 'holy' in his character, something impossible if he was conceived in the normal way (see Psalm 51:5; Ephesians 2:3). He was to be without human failure because he was to be without a human father. In a way true of no other person, he would be called 'the Son of God' (v.35).

The mystery is accepted

However marvellous all this sounded to Mary, it remained staggeringly mysterious. Yet at the end of the day, she accepted it all. Her final words to the angel were 'I am the Lord's servant. May it be to me as you have said' (v.38). There were many things she could not understand, but nothing that she was not prepared to accept. There is an important lesson here for all Christians. We are not always clear as to what God is doing with our lives. God's ways are mysterious and walking in them can sometimes be perplexing or painful. Yet we are called upon always to submit to his 'good, pleasing and perfect will' (Romans 12:2) — whatever that might mean — in order that God might be glorified and Christ exalted. Even the question of whether we live or die then becomes immaterial! (See Philippians 1:20.)

'As for God, his way is perfect' (Psalm 18:30).

--- **4** ---

Magnificat!

Luke 1:39-56

Our last study ended with Mary humbly submitting to the angel Gabriel's astonishing message. Yet the whole experience must have been a very testing one and Mary decided to take a three months' break at Elizabeth's home in the hill country of Judea (vv.39-40,56). Today's reading covers all we know of their time together.

The welcome Elizabeth gave

The setting is very warm and friendly, with two mothers-to-be sharing those things nearest to their hearts. Yet there is profound spiritual truth locked up in it all. The first thing that stands out in Elizabeth's welcome is that she showed no jealousy whatever. She immediately acknowledged Mary as being 'blessed. . . among women' (v.42). Elizabeth was older and had herself been greatly honoured by God, but she did not make any capital out of these facts. Instead she counted herself unworthy even to receive Mary as a guest (v.43). Notice how closely this compares with what Elizabeth's son John was to say about Jesus many years later (see Matthew 3:14). Finally, Elizabeth's welcome showed that she had great faith. She was not only absolutely certain that God would perform all that he had promised (v.45), but she also believed that Mary's unborn child was her own 'Lord' (v.43). The reason for Elizabeth's spirituality and

insight is not hard to find — she was 'filled with the Holy
Spirit' (v.41).

The worship Mary offered

The section containing verses 46-55 is sometimes called
the *Magnificat* (from the Latin of the opening words) and
is still sung in churches all over the world today. In it we
can trace at least three of the attributes of God. Firstly,
there is *his majesty* (vv.46,47,49). Make a special note of
the fact that Mary acknowledged God as her Saviour
(v.47), which meant that she knew herself to be a sinner.
What shines out from this passage is not the sinlessness
of Mary, but the sovereign majesty of God, of whom
alone it can be said, 'Holy is his name' (v.49). Secondly,
we see *the tremendous power of God* (v.49). Mary began on a
personal level, and said that God had done 'great things'
for her (v.49); but then she moved on to the much wider
truth that God had 'performed mighty deeds with his
arm' (v.51). Nobody has a correct view of the world or of
history until they can see that God is constantly and
sovereignly at work. Mary then developed this overall
truth in two ways: *God exalts and humbles* (vv.51,52); all
kings and kingdoms are under God's sovereign control,
and even the worst of despots is subject to his power (link
Psalm 22:28 and Proverbs 8:15 with Exodus 9:16). *God
enriches and impoverishes* (v.53); if it pleases God's purposes
he can bring a millionaire to the breadline and place a
pauper in a palace. Our health and wealth are in God's
hands, which is why Paul was able to say what he did at
Philippians 4:11,12. Thirdly, we see the *wonderful mercy of
God* (vv.50,54,55). Notice that God's mercy is said to be
based on his Word: it is 'even as he said to our fathers'
(v.55). The Old Testament promises must have seemed
just ancient history to many of the Jews, but God had not
forgotten and in helping his people he was 'remembering
to be merciful' (v.54) and Mary saw what was about to
happen as the fulfilment of God's pledge to bless his

people. God's promises are just as real today. Isaiah
55:6,7 and 2 Chronicles 7:14 are two wonderful
examples, but notice the conditions attached! God will
always add his blessing to man's repentance and
obedience.

'Glorify the Lord with me; let us exalt his name together' (Psalm
34:3).

5

Benedictus!

Luke 1:57-80

In today's reading, Luke completes setting the scene for
the coming of the Messiah by describing the events
surrounding the birth of John, which took place a little
earlier. The passage divides very naturally into an
introduction and a benediction.

Introduction
Luke takes up the story when 'it was time for Elizabeth
to have her baby' (v.57). Primarily, of course, he meant
that she gave birth about nine months after conception,
but the fuller meaning is that John arrived exactly
according to God's schedule. Elizabeth was proving to
the hilt the kind of promise made in Joshua 23:14. When
the happy event took place, her neighbours and relatives
'shared her joy' (v.58) — a welcome change of spirit from
verse 25! According to Old Testament law, male children
were circumcised on the eighth day (Genesis 17:12). This

was also the day when the child would be named. People assumed that he would be called Zechariah, after his father (that seems to be the meaning of the end of v.59); but Elizabeth interrupted them to say that he was to be called John (v.60). They were obviously puzzled about this and turned to Zechariah for his choice (vv.61,62). To their amazement, he immediately wrote, 'His name is John' (v.63). By now he had obviously realized that God was in this whole matter and that his responsibility was unqualified obedience to the clear instructions he had been given (see v.13). Immediately the result of his disobedience was removed (v.64); God did not press his judgement against him a moment longer than was necessary. In turn, Zechariah's first words were of praise and worship (vv.67,68; compare Noah's actions in Genesis 8:18-20 immediately after the flood had subsided).

Benediction

Zechariah's words are sometimes called the *Benedictus* (the Latin of the opening phrase). The first thing for which Zechariah gave thanks was that God had 'come and . . . redeemed his people'. Although he must at that moment have been the proudest father in Israel, the subject of his praise was not John but Jesus! His great theme was that God had at last fulfilled his promise and that the Messiah had come (though Jesus was still in his mother's womb at the time). He then used several vivid phrases to describe the coming child and to show what amazing things he was to accomplish. For instance, he would be 'a horn of salvation' (v.69) — the horn being a symbol of strength — and as such he would save his people from their enemies (v.71). No human mind can grasp the tremendous power needed to deliver even one person from the guilt and grip of sin, yet Jesus was to do this for countless multitudes. Then he was described as 'the Most High' and 'the Lord' (v.76), titles which could

only speak of deity; and it was because of this that he
was able to fulfil God's covenant promises (vv.72,73).
Thirdly, he was given the title 'the rising sun. . . from
heaven' (v.78); and as such he would 'shine on those
living in darkness and in the shadow of death' (v.79).
Compare this with what Jesus himself said later (John
8:12) and with what Paul added at 2 Corinthians 4:3,4.
As the sun gives light to the earth, so Jesus gives light to
the soul. Yet a personal response is called for. The
purpose of our deliverance by Christ is that we might
'serve him without fear in holiness and righteousness
before him all our days' (vv.74,75). Read that quotation
through again — slowly! — and try to grasp something
of the depth of response which your salvation demands.
God's claims on the redeemed sinner are moral, spiritual
and *total*!

*'For you were once darkness, but now you are light in the Lord.
Live as children of light'* (Ephesians 5:8).

6

God breaks through

Luke 2:1-20

Having carefully sketched in the background as part of
the account he was writing to Theophilus, Luke now sets
out to describe the stupendous event which turned the
tide of history, the moment when God broke into the
world in a unique and astonishing way. We can draw the
threads of Luke's record together in three paragraphs.

The edict from Rome

Luke begins by timing things in the context of other events. In this case, he notes the fact that the Roman emperor, Caesar Augustus, had 'issued a decree that a census should be taken of the entire Roman world' (v.1) and adds that one particular census took place 'while Quirinius was governor of Syria' (v.2). These censuses were taken every fourteen years, the results being used mainly for taxation purposes. Yet the emperor's edict, together with all the local administrative arrangements, were now to fit perfectly into God's plan. People were required to register in their own home town (v.3), which for Joseph meant a long journey from Nazareth to Bethlehem, the capital city of Judea (v.4). By this time, he had married Mary (see Matthew 1:24,25) and her baby was due very soon (v.5). Normally she might have been excused this long journey, but there was nothing normal about this particular situation! Hundreds of years before, God had decreed that the Messiah would be born in Bethlehem (see Micah 5:2); the last of the pieces was now falling perfectly into place! The actual birth of Jesus is recorded in a handful of words. With the town full of visitors taking part in the Roman census, even an expectant mother had to take whatever accommodation she could find (vv.6,7).

The message from heaven

Meantime, other people were going about their normal business, and these included shepherds guarding their flocks in the nearby fields (v.8). Suddenly, they were dazzled and terrified by the appearance of an angel (v.9). But the angel brought 'good news of great joy' (v.10). That very day, a child had been born in Bethlehem who was 'Saviour', 'Christ' and 'Lord' (v.11). The word 'Christ' is the Greek word for 'Messiah' and the word 'Lord' was used as God's own name; to bring both names together put the new-born child's identity beyond all doubt! God himself had broken into history in a way that would affect 'all the people' (v.10). This mighty Saviour was to transform the lives of multitudes; and the day will come when his praises will be sung by those 'purchased. . . for God. . . from every tribe and language and people and nation' (Revelation 5:9). No wonder a great army of angels suddenly surrounded the shepherds, praising God and promising that there would be peace on earth 'to men on whom his favour rests' (v.14).

The news from Bethlehem
The shepherds were not given instructions to visit Jesus, but the angels obviously assumed they would (v.12) and they did (vv.15,16). Shepherds were among the lowest paid of the working classes and in some ways were social outcasts. Yet they were chosen by God to be among the very first people to see the infant Jesus. What is more, they were also among the first evangelists of his birth (v.17). Even when they returned to their normal place of work, they could not keep their experience to themselves, but shared it in a spirit of praise and worship (v.20). They were not professional preachers or gifted scholars; but they could share what they knew! Look up Acts 4.20. Do you feel like that? When did you last tell someone about Christ?

'For the grace of God that brings salvation has appeared to all men' (Titus 2:11).

—————————— **7** ——————————

Nunc Dimittis!

Luke 2:21-40

Luke has already described the day when John was circumcised and named (1:59,60). He now records the same moment in the life of Jesus, a day marked, as was John's, by extraordinary statements of divine truth. Basically, two very significant things happened.

The law was fulfilled

As we have already seen, circumcision was in accordance with Jewish law (Genesis 17:12). As with John, the choice of the child's name did not rest with the parents; there had been specific instructions from God (see Matthew 1:21). The name 'Jesus' was in common use (see Colossians 4:11), but in this case the naming of the child was both miraculous and full of meaning. The word 'Jesus' means 'God is salvation' and was therefore the perfect human name for man's divine Saviour. Another Jewish law taught that every first-born son was consecrated to God (link v.23 with Exodus 13:2,12,15). This was a reminder of God's goodness in sparing the Jews when he destroyed the first-born of the Egyptians (see Exodus 12:29). The law went on to say that the child must then be symbolically 'redeemed' by the payment of five shekels (see Numbers 18:15,16), and in order to do this Joseph and Mary took Jesus to Jerusalem (v.22).

Yet another law concerned the purification of the

mother. After the birth of a male child, the mother was ceremonially unclean for forty days (see Leviticus 12:1-4), after which she must offer 'a year-old lamb for a burnt offering and a young pigeon or a dove for a sin offering' (Leviticus 12:6). If she could not afford a lamb, a second pigeon or dove would be sufficient. The priest would then sacrifice the animals and pronounce the woman clean (see Leviticus 12:8). In the light of this, verse 24 tells us something about Joseph and Mary's financial position. In all of these details, Jesus was identified with those he himself had come to redeem (link v.38 with Galatians 4:4).

The Lord was revealed
Also in Jerusalem was a godly man called Simeon, who longed for the coming of the Messiah and had been given a remarkable promise that he would see him before he died (vv.25,26). Led by the Holy Spirit, he was in the temple when Joseph and Mary entered (v.27). As soon as he saw Jesus, he took him in his arms and praised God in words sometimes called the *Nunc Dimittis* (the opening words in Latin). As with the hymns of Mary and Zechariah, the great theme of Simeon's song was 'salvation' (v.30) which was to be announced to 'all people' and would be a blessing both to Jews and Gentiles (v.32). Simeon was so sure that Jesus was the Messiah that he would gladly have died there and then! (v.29) Joseph and Mary were amazed that this stranger should know such things (v.33). Then Simeon made these prophecies about Jesus: he would mean damnation to some and salvation to others; he would meet great opposition; men's reactions to him would reveal their true spiritual condition, and something (obviously his death) would cause great sorrow to Mary (check all of this with vv.34,35). Immediately after this, a devout old prophetess called Anna came up to them and gave thanks to God. After this one brief encounter, she

constantly spoke about Jesus to all those who were
eagerly waiting for the Messiah to come (vv.36-38). For
her, as for Simeon, the wait was over!

This is Anna's only appearance in the Bible, but what
a challenge she presents! Worship, fasting, prayer,
thanksgiving and constant testimony about Christ —
and all this by someone at least eighty-four years old.
Can you begin to match her faithfulness and enthusiasm?

'Go. . . and tell. . . how much the Lord has done for you' (Mark
5:19).

8

Spiritual wisdom

Luke 2:41-52

One of the most unusual things about the biography of
Jesus is that from an ordinary human viewpoint it seems
so uneven. There are about three chapters dealing with
the events surrounding his birth and then almost nothing
for about thirty years. The only incident recorded about
Jesus between his babyhood and his manhood is the one
contained in today's reading, when Jesus was twelve
years old (v.42). In the course of our previous study we
noticed that Mary and Joseph were devout and disciplined in their religion (glance back to v.39 again). As
such, they would piously seek to keep all the established
requirements regarding attendance at the great Jewish
festivals. The law required all males to attend three times
a year — at the Feast of Unleavened Bread (or the

Passover), at Pentecost and at the Feast of Tabernacles
(see Exodus 23:14-17). This is the background to what
we read in verses 41,42. The family was in Jerusalem in
compliance with the law of God, on this occasion to
celebrate the Passover, which commemorated the
Israelites' deliverance from the Egyptians (see Exodus
12:1-14).

Misunderstanding

The festival lasted a week (see Exodus 13:6) and when it
was over the party from Nazareth started for home
(v.43). We are not told how many people travelled
together on the excursion from Nazareth, but the group
was obviously large enough for Mary and Joseph to
travel all day without being particularly concerned that
they had not seen Jesus since they left the city. It was
only at the end of the day that they realized their mistake
(v.44). A Christian can make the same kind of careless
mistake with regard to his spiritual condition. Revelation
3:17 can be deeply challenging on this point! Never be
satisfied with 'supposing' that the Lord is with you in
life's decisions and directions. The right attitude for a
safe and happy journey is found in 2 Peter 1:1-10!

Understanding

Having failed to find Jesus among their relatives and
friends (v.45), the distraught parents made their way
back to Jerusalem. When they eventually found him, he
was in the temple, engaged in deep discussion with the
leading religious teachers of the day. Although Jesus was
not even a teenager, the scholars were 'amazed at his
understanding and his answers' (v.47). By his searching
questions and superb answers Jesus showed himself to
have a grasp of spiritual matters far beyond his years.
Colossians 2:3 explains why!

No understanding
In spite of all they had seen and heard at the time of his birth, Joseph and Mary were baffled by all of this; they were 'astonished' (v.48). Mary blamed Jesus for getting lost, rather then accepting the blame for losing him (v.48), and they obviously did not understand what he meant by saying, 'I had to be in my Father's house' (v.49). As we saw in our previous study, a developing knowledge of God's will and ways is essential if life is to make any real sense. Without this spiritual understanding life becomes clouded and confusing. Incidentally, make careful note that in this passage we have Jesus' first recorded words (in v.49). They tell us that Jesus already sensed his special relationship to God and the need for his whole-hearted commitment and obedience. His greatest wisdom lay there — and the lesson should be obvious!

'The fear of the Lord is the beginning of wisdom' (Psalm 111:10).

--------------- **9** ---------------

The P.R. man

Luke 3:1-20

Having given us one fascinating glimpse of Jesus as he approached his teenage years and told us in a phrase or two about his disciplined and spiritual family life at Nazareth (look back to the last two verses of the previous chapter), Luke now resumes the story of 'John, son of

Zechariah' (v.2). The last mention of John had been
about eighteen years earlier; all we know of him in the
meantime is what we read in 1:80. Now it was time for
John's public ministry to begin, and Luke, with his usual
attention to detail, dates this with great accuracy
(vv.1,2). In modern language, we might call John a
public relations man. As he himself made very clear, his
one great task in life was to point people to Jesus (see
John 1:8,29,30). Three phrases help us to sum up his
ministry.

The mission he prized
Elsewhere the Bible tells us that John was 'a man who
was sent from God' (John 1:6); here, we are told that
'The word of God came to John' (v.2). What is more, his
ministry was itself the fulfilment of prophecy (link vv.4,5
with Isaiah 40:3,4). There had not been a prophet in the
land for 400 years, but John was the honoured successor
of all those in the Old Testament. Later, Paul was to
remind all Christians, 'We are therefore Christ's ambassadors' (2 Corinthians 5:20), another honoured title
carrying the same kind of responsibility. How highly do
you prize the position in which God has placed you in the
world? And how seriously do you carry out your duties?

The message he preached
In a nutshell, this was 'a baptism of repentance for the
forgiveness of sins' (v.3), and when crowds flocked to be
baptized (v.7) John made it clear that repentance came
first: he told people to 'produce fruit in keeping with
repentance' (v.8.) He was more interested in examining
hearts than in counting heads — a lesson for all
Christian workers today! He then pressed home the
urgency of his message by saying, 'The axe is already at
the root of the trees' (v.9) and that if there was no good
fruit judgement would follow. When specific groups
asked him how this life of repentance applied to them, his

answers were clear and forthright. One group of people were told to be open-hearted and kind (v.11); the tax-collectors were to be scrupulously honest (v.13); the soldiers were to act with absolute integrity (v.14). Christians are expected to have the highest living standards in the world!

The Master he proclaimed

We have already seen that Isaiah's prophecy pin-pointed John's ministry as being to 'prepare the way for the Lord' (v.4) and when people were 'waiting expectantly and were all wondering in their hearts if John might possibly be the Christ' (v.15) he made it quite clear that he was merely the forerunner of 'one more powerful than I' (v.16). *His* baptism would be 'with the Holy Spirit and with fire' (v.16). There may be a link here with Malachi 3:1-3, in which case the picture is that of the Holy Spirit purging and purifying the life of the Christian with the purpose of making him more and more like Christ. For those unwilling to submit to the fire of cleansing, there would one day be the fire of judgement (v.17). John's fearless preaching against the specific sins of Herod Antipas, the ruler of Galilee, eventually landed him in prison (vv.19,20) but he remained faithful to his commission — a P.R. man for Jesus!

The world in which we live is never going to be a bed of roses for the faithful Christian. Being faithful to God and his standards needs a cool head and a courageous heart — and God can give you both!

'So do not be ashamed to testify about our Lord' (2 Timothy 1:8).

10

Just a list of names?

Luke 3:21-38

In the passage covered by our last study, Luke brought us up-to-date with the story of John the Baptist, telling us of the beginning of his public ministry and then jumping ahead to tell us that he was eventually sent to prison for his outspoken denunciation of Herod's sins (vv.19,20). Now Luke brings the real subject of his biography back into the picture (v.21). Matthew tells us that John was reluctant to baptize Jesus, but Jesus insisted that this was the right thing to do (see Matthew 3:14,15). Although without any sin of his own, Jesus identified himself with the sinners he came to save. The remarkable 'appearance' of the Holy Spirit and the audible voice from heaven must have made this an astonishing moment for all who were there! But most of today's reading is taken up with Jesus' genealogical table or family tree. Yet even this is part of God's Word and therefore of value to us (see 2 Timothy 3:16). The list of names tells us three things about Jesus.

It shows his humanity
The fact that Jesus *had* a family tree shows that he was not a figment of the imagination or a kind of mythological half-man-half-god. He was by turns a baby, a child, a teenager and a mature man; he 'grew in wisdom and stature' (Luke 2:52). He knew what it was to be

hungry (Luke 4:2), thirsty (John 4:7) and tired (John 4:6). He was neither superman, supermyth, nor superstar. Jesus came to earth 'in human likeness' (Philippians 2:7). One of the many great truths which follow is that he now intimately understands the problems and pressures that face us day by day. Hebrews 4:15 brings this out very well, and Hebrews 4:16 tells us what to do as a result.

It supports his authority

The Jewish priests began their public ministry 'from thirty years old' (see Numbers 4:47), and Jesus chose the same moment to begin his (v.23). Yet if he was really the Messiah he would need to be able to prove his direct descent from King David (link Jeremiah 23:5, 2 Samuel 7:12,13 with Acts 2:29,30; 13:22,23). Now notice how, even before his birth, the angel spoke of Jesus being given 'the throne of his father David' (see 1:32). And here, in his family tree, the last name in verse 31 slots right into place! Even by 'natural' means, the claims Jesus later made to be the Messiah had exactly the support they needed.

It suggests his divinity

The final man mentioned in the family tree is Adam and he is described as 'the son of God'. This would normally mean that Jesus was in direct line of created descent, but notice how precisely this error is avoided. In verse 23 Luke speaks of Jesus as being 'the son, so it was thought, of Joseph'. This was what people *thought* (look up Matthew 13:55, for instance) but they were mistaken. He was the son of Mary, but not of Joseph. The angel's message to Mary made it clear that the conception of Jesus in the womb would be the miraculous work of the Holy Spirit (see 1:35) and now, at the beginning of his public ministry, God announces him to be 'my Son, whom I love' (v.22). The family tree suggests that Jesus was more than a mere man; the New Testament as a whole makes it clear that he was no less than God!

Today's reading may not have seemed very exciting, but it should be a great faith-strengthener. It confirms that Jesus understands your needs, burdens, problems and stresses because he was human, and that he can help you to face them today because he is divine.

'. . . *a descendant of David. . . declared with power to be the Son of God*' (Romans 1:3,4).

11

Triumphant in temptation

Luke 4:1-13

These opening verses of Luke 4 contain what must surely be one of the most remarkable passages in the whole Bible. Although the language is very simple, and the whole section itself less than 200 words in length, it records a direct confrontation between Jesus and the devil. The subject of the whole passage is temptation and because this is something so real to every Christian in the world we should study these words with great care. One of the greatest lessons comes across in the opening verse, where we are told that Jesus was 'full of the Holy Spirit' and that he was 'led by the Spirit in the desert' (v.1). This shows us very clearly that when a person is severely tempted it does *not* mean that he is living a sub-standard life. Jesus was fiercely tempted throughout his earthly life, yet at no point was he less than perfect. Note

Hebrews 4:15 very carefully. With that truth clearly in our minds we can now look in detail at the temptations Jesus faced at this particular point in his life.

They were diverse
Notice how the devil switched his point of attack. Firstly, there were six weeks of unspecified but uninterrupted assaults (notice that at verse 2). Then the devil tried to capitalize on a physical weakness, the fact that Jesus was hungry (v.3). Next, he attempted the predictable avenue of pride (vv.5-7). Finally, he tempted Jesus to misuse his unique relationship to his heavenly Father and, though out of context, to stretch God's promises to cover personal folly (vv.9-11). In this third temptation the devil even had the audacity to quote the Bible (see Psalm 91:11,12). Let this be a lesson to us all! The devil has a thousand ways in which to attack the Christian and he is capable of switching tactics with bewildering speed. Learn the discipline of being on your guard at all times. Matthew 26:41 contains the Christian soldier's Orders for the Day!

They were deceptive
Look through these three temptations again and notice how *attractive* they all were. By yielding to the first, Jesus could have ended the pangs of hunger from which he was suffering. By yielding to the second, he could have set up an immediate earthly kingdom. By yielding to the third, he could have become a superstar overnight. But had he yielded at any of these points his whole life's mission would have collapsed. No wonder Paul speaks of 'the devil's schemes' (Ephesians 6:11) and that Jesus warned us plainly that 'When [the devil] lies, he speaks his native language. . .' (John 8:44). Temptation always promises more than it produces. There may be pleasure in sin, as Hebrews 11:25 admits quite openly, but there is never satisfaction. Study this whole subject carefully and

aim to be able to say what Paul did at the end of 2 Corinthians 2:11!

They were defeated
Surrounded as we are by temptations of every kind, it is a great encouragement to read that when Jesus had firmly and successfully resisted all of these attacks, the devil 'left him' (v.13). Even so, we must also note that he only went away 'until an opportune time' (v.13). In the same way, we dare not think that victory over one attack means immunity from any other. Notice, too, that the devil was defeated not by a histrionic display of supernatural power, but by a right use of Scripture (look at vv.4,8,12) and because Jesus was filled with the Holy Spirit. He left the wilderness as he entered it 'in the power of the Spirit' (v.14). Victory over every temptation *is* possible, as 1 Corinthians 10:13 makes clear, but only in the combined power of the holy Scriptures and the Holy Spirit.

'Submit yourselves, then, to God. Resist the devil, and he will flee from you' (James 4:7).

12

The voice of the people. . .

Luke 4:14-30

After the ordeal in the wilderness Jesus moved up country to Galilee (v.14) and settled for a while in his home town of Nazareth (v.16). In the course of today's

reading Luke makes one brief comment on his ministry
in general and then gives us a more detailed description
of one incident at Nazareth in particular. If we put these
two sections of the narrative together, we can listen to the
reaction of the people of his day to the life and teaching of
Jesus.

Praise

When Jesus began preaching in the local Galilean
synagogues, news of his ministry 'spread through the
whole countryside' (v.14), and before long 'everyone
praised him' (v.15). At this particular point in the story
we are not given any specific details as to either the
words or the actions which sparked off such enthusiasm,
but it is surely not difficult to imagine the situation. He
had come into Galilee 'in the power of the Spirit' (v.14)
and this must surely have meant that his dynamic
ministry was in vivid contrast to a great deal of deadness
among local congregations. Everybody who seeks to lead
others in worship should constantly pray to be delivered
from the dreadful drudgery of 'services as usual' and to
be liberated into the place where God speaks and people
sit up and take notice. If only all today's preachers and
teachers were able to say what Paul did in 1 Corinthians
2:4!

Prejudice

It is important to notice in passing that Jesus was a
regular worshipper in his local church (link v.16 with
Hebrews 10:25). When on this particular occasion he got
to his feet to read the Scriptures, he was handed a scroll
containing part of Isaiah's prophecy (v.17). He then read
a brief passage (compare vv.18,19 with Isaiah 61:1,2),
rolled up the scroll and sat down (v.20). As this was the
normal position for a preacher, 'The eyes of everyone in
the synagogue were fastened on him' (v.20), obviously
waiting to hear what this remarkable man had to say. If

they expected a sensation, they were not disappointed, because his opening words were 'Today this scripture is fulfilled in your hearing' (v.21). In the plainest way he claimed to be the living fulfilment of Isaiah's ancient prophecy, in other words to be the Messiah. While the people were forced to admire his 'gracious words', they could still only think of him as a young man from their own town (v.22). In a smaller way, we will sometimes face the same kind of prejudice and this is especially likely to happen at home or at work. But in some cases, it will be because people do not like Christianity at close quarters!

Persecution

Anticipating that they would ask for some startling proof of his claim (compare v.23 with Matthew 12:38; 16:1) Jesus condemned their built-in prejudice with a proverb (v.24). He might have got away with that, but he then went on to give two Old Testament illustrations of Jews rejecting genuine prophets. In the first, Elijah was helped, not by Jews but by a foreigner from Zarephath in Sidon (link vv.25,26 with 1 Kings 17:1-9). In the second, there is no record of Elisha healing any of the many lepers in Israel, yet he gladly helped the Syrian army captain Naaman (link v.27 with 2 Kings 5:1-14). This triggered off a furious reaction, with the members of the congregation so enraged that they tried to throw him over a nearby cliff (v.29). But in a quiet display of magnificent authority he simply 'walked right through the crowd and went on his way' (v.30). No Christian can avoid persecution of one kind or another, but 2 Corintians 4:17,18 puts it all into perspective!

'Everyone who wants to live a godly life in Christ Jesus will be persecuted' (2 Timothy 3:12).

13

. . . And the voice of God

Luke 4:31-44

Moving on from Nazareth (which we never hear of him visiting again), Jesus went to Capernaum, on the northern shore of the Sea of Galilee, and continued his preaching, including regular ministry in the synagogues throughout the whole area of Judea (vv.31,44). Luke obviously condenses an extended period of ministry into a few verses, but this only serves to emphasize the fact that these days were packed with dynamic action. And it was not just action, but *divine* action. Luke is not just reporting the spectacular progress of an enthusiastic young preacher. Here is *God* on the loose, sweeping into one situation after another and transforming them through the words spoken by his Son. In our last study we heard the voice of the people — a disappointing mixture of praise, prejudice and persecution. In this passage we can listen to the voice of God, the impact of which can be summed up in four paragrahs.

Doctrine was revealed
People were amazed at the teaching of Jesus 'because his message had authority' (v.32). Religious teachers were two a penny at that time, but Jesus was different (see Matthew 7:29 for the way in which this contrast was expressed on another occasion). Others groped for the truth; Jesus revealed it, both in his words and in his

life (see John 14:6). Titus 2:10 says something very significant to us in this whole area of the relationship between life and truth.

Demons were rebuked

It is extraordinary to notice how the evil spirits recognized Jesus (vv.34,41) — a sobering reminder of their supernatural intelligence. Yet their knowledge produced only fear and terror (compare v.34 with James 2:19). With majestic authority Jesus rebuked them again and again (vv.35,41). Evil spirits are still actively at work today and demon possession is still a terrible reality with appalling effects on individuals and society. But however terrifying the powers of evil may be, the Christian can rejoice in knowing that his Saviour and Lord is one whose superiority is such that he is able to say, 'All authority in heaven and on earth has been given to me' (Matthew 28:18). Make a careful note of how emphatically this same great truth is expressed at 1 Peter 3:22.

Disease was removed

From the synagogue Jesus went to Simon Peter's house, where his mother-in-law was 'suffering from a high fever' (v.38). This is a vivid medical phrase; Colossians 4:14 tells us why Luke was qualified to use it. At the request of those present, Jesus rebuked the disease — just as he had the demons! — and her temperature quickly dropped to normal (v.39). All disease is primarily the result of sin — though not always *directly* so (see John 9:1-3) — and is therefore subordinate to the power of God. While God uses the body's natural mechanism, drugs, medicine and medical skill to restore people to health today, he also works directly and by miraculous means. Do we limit God by locking this kind of healing away within the covers of the Bible?

Duty was required

It is lovely to notice that as soon as Peter's mother-in-law
had been healed she started attending to the needs of
others (v.39). Later, Jesus told those who wanted to
detain him that he must go elsewhere to preach 'the good
news of the kingdom of God' (v.43). The fact that the
Lord is King *is* good news, but it also demands
obedience, duty and service. Paul called himself 'a
servant of God' (Titus 1:1). As a Christian, you share
the same high privilege — and the same searching
responsibility.

'Today, if you hear [God's] voice, do not harden your hearts'
(Psalm 95:7,8).

14

Jesus is Lord

Luke 5:1-16

Today's reading continues Luke's account of the public
ministry of Jesus in the general area of Judea. The
passage divides itself very clearly into two separate
incidents, one by the 'Lake of Gennesaret', that is the Sea
of Galilee (v.1), and the other in an unnamed town
(v.12). Each of the incidents centres on a miracle
performed by Jesus, the first demonstrating his mastery
over nature and the second demonstrating his mastery
over the human body. Later in the New Testament we
are shown that one of the earliest and simplest con-
fessions of a Christian's faith was 'Jesus is Lord'

(Romans 10:9). That truth comes across loud and clear
as we read this part of Luke's account of Christ's words
and actions.

Unqualified obedience

The numbers of people following Jesus were growing all
the time and the chapter opens with 'the people
crowding around him and listening to the word of God'
(v.1). Indeed, the crowds were so large that Jesus had to
think of some means of ensuring that they could all see
and hear him. Seeing two fishing-boats drawn up by the
lake, he climbed into one of them (the one belonging to
Simon Peter) and asked him to put out a little from the
shore. The result was an ideal pulpit from which he was
able to be seen and heard clearly (vv.2,3). When he had
finished teaching the people, Jesus asked Peter to sail
into deeper water in order to catch some fish (v.4). To an
experienced Galilean fisherman, the idea was absurd.
After all, they had worked hard all night and caught
nothing (v.5). If the experts had drawn a blank during
prime fishing time, what chance did they stand at the
worst time of day? Yet Peter's doubts were immediately
overtaken by his willingness to obey: '*Because you say so,* I
will let down the nets' (v.5). Here is a vital principle
for every Christian's life, because in practical terms,
Christianity *is* obedience. Repentance, faith, prayer,
witnessing, love, kindness, humility, holiness — all of
these are commanded and are therefore part of the
believer's basic duty. The Bible's overall message to the
Christian is Mary's word to the disciples at Cana: 'Do
whatever he tells you' (John 2:5). Are you being
consciously obedient to all of God's revealed will to you?
The outcome of Peter's obedience was amazing — his
ship was filled with fish (v.7), his heart was filled with
worship (v.8 and link this with Isaiah 6:5) and his life
was filled with service! (v.11)

Unmerited compassion

In Bible times, sufferers from leprosy were literally avoided like the plague. They were forced to live in isolation while their bodies rotted away. Lepers were written off as unclean, defiled, unwanted. Yet when a man in an advanced state of the disease —we are told that he was 'covered with leprosy' (v.12) — flung himself at the feet of Jesus and cried, 'Lord, if you are willing, you can make me clean' (v.12), Jesus did both the unthinkable and the impossible: he *touched* him and said, 'I am willing. Be clean!' (v.13) The man was healed immediately (v.13) and Jesus told him to fulfil the Old Testament requirement for obtaining a clean bill of health from the priest (link v.14 with Leviticus 14:7). This deeply moving incident is a beautiful illustration of Christ's mission in the world. Man is full of the leprosy of sin and (even worse than in the physical equivalent) he is fully deserving of the death it brings (Romans 5:12). Yet if he is willing to repent of his sin he will discover that Jesus is willing to touch him and heal him — notice how beautifully John 3:17 fits in with 2 Peter 3:9! As Christians, too, we need to open our lives in every part to the Lord's 'I am willing', in order to be 'filled to the measure of all the fulness of God' (Ephesians 3:19).

'His hands. . . heal' (Job 5:18).

—————————— **15** ——————————

Men who met the Master

Luke 5:17-39

In reading the Gospels we are, of course, reading the
nearest thing we have to a biography of Jesus and it is
therefore to be expected that he holds the centre of the
stage. But we can also learn a great deal by focusing
some of our attention on the other people involved in the
narrative as it unfolds. Their actions and attitudes can
teach us a great deal, often. by way of example or
warning. Today's passage, which contains three separate
incidents, is a good illustration of this.

The man who was cured
By now Jesus was mobbed wherever he went, people
coming from miles around to listen to his teaching (v.17).
In the middle of one indoor session, certain men (we are
told at Mark 2:3 that there were four of them) brought a
paralysed friend on his sleeping mat and tried to get him
to Jesus. Unable to get through the crowd, they carried
him up the outside steps to the flat roof, broke it open
and let the sick man down through the hole they had
made (v.19). Jesus' immediate response was not to heal
him, but to forgive him (v.20), an action which immediately caused the scribes and Pharisees to level a charge of
blasphemy at him for claiming to do something that was
God's prerogative (v.21). In reply, Jesus asked them a
question: did they think it easier to pronounce words of

forgiveness or of healing? (v.23) The point behind the question is that the first would seem to be easier, because the other would need an *obvious* miracle to prove that the words had been effective. Without waiting for their answer, Jesus proceeded to add the 'difficult' word (v.24) and the man was cured in an instant (v.25) with the result that 'Everyone was amazed and gave praise to God' (v.26). But notice one very important phrase: Jesus acted when he 'saw their faith' (v.20). The whole incident hinges on this. Are you proving promises like the one at Matthew 17:20, or praying along the lines of Luke 17:5?

The man who was called

Levi (also known as Matthew — see Matthew 9:9) was a civil servant working in the local tax office (v.27). When Jesus said to him, 'Follow me' (v.27), his response was immediate and whole-hearted (v.28). What is more, he arranged an evangelistic dinner (that same night?) inviting many of his unconverted colleagues and friends to meet Jesus (v.29). The religious die-hards did not approve of a religious teacher mixing with outsiders, but Jesus put them neatly in their place with two unanswerable comments (vv.31,32). The obvious challenge of Matthew's call is one of happy boldness in sharing his faith with others. An Old Testament prophet had caught the same spirit (see Isaiah 63:7). Have you?

The men who were confused

Some people were puzzled as to why the followers of Jesus did not make fasting part of their religion, as did the followers of John the Baptist (v.33). In reply, Jesus said that wedding guests did not fast in the bridegroom's presence (v.34) — notice that John the Baptist used the same joyful picture of his relationship to Jesus (John 3:29). He then gave a veiled prophecy of his death, after which fasting would be appropriate (v.35). The two tiny

parables that followed (vv.36-39) both pointed out
the same truth — the Christian life is exhilarating
and dynamic and cannot be contained in worn-out
structures. The lesson for us is that we should let our
approach to Christian life and witness be as fresh as the
Christian message itself. Clinging to familiar, com-
fortable customs can sometimes hinder the dynamic
growth which should characterize the believer's life.
When it is right to do so be prepared to let them go, and
to move on.

'Blessed are those who have not seen and yet have believed' (John
20;29).

16

The Lord!

Luke 6:1-16

As Jesus continued his ministry, the Pharisees, a strictly
orthodox Jewish sect, continued to find fault with the
way he did things. As we shall see several times in these
studies, his behaviour on the sabbath was a particularly
frequent bone of contention. In this passage he deals
with two criticisms levelled at him and chooses twelve
apostles, and in doing so shows himself to be the Lord.

Lord of the sabbath

The disciples' actions in verse 1 seem harmless enough
to us, but they were not to the Pharisees. This particular
interpretation of religious laws was so detailed and

absurd that plucking corn was equivalent to reaping; rubbing the corn in the hand was threshing; picking out the kernels from the husks (which the disciples must have done before eating them) was winnowing, and the whole process meant that they had in effect engaged in the work of preparing food for eating! This was their line of thinking and it meant that in their eyes the disciples were religious criminals engaged in wholesale law-breaking. Such blatant wickedness could not go unchallenged, so they bluntly demanded, 'Why are you doing what is unlawful on the Sabbath?' (v.2) In reply, Jesus quoted an Old Testament incident (link vv.3,4 with 1 Samuel 21:1-6) in which David (one of their great heroes) and his men had once asked for, and been given by the priest, bread solemnly set aside for the priests' exclusive use in accordance with Leviticus 24:5-9. The inference was that if David's need took preference over established ceremonial law, the disciples' hunger (see Matthew 12:1) must surely take precedence over the Pharisees' ridiculous interpretation of the law of Moses. What is more, Jesus went on to claim that he was 'Lord of the Sabbath' (v.5), with the obvious inference that he was not subject to any man-made additions to the divine law. On another sabbath, Jesus was confronted in the synagogue by a man with a withered hand (v.6). Notice that the careful Dr Luke even tells us which hand it was! Sensing that Jesus might take action to heal the man, the Pharisees were ready to pounce again (v.7). But Jesus forestalled them with an unanswerable question (v.9), which again appealed to mercy as a law which should come first — see what he calls it in Matthew 23:23. Getting no answer, Jesus promptly healed the man (v.10), but the Pharisees were so bigoted that they raged when they should have rejoiced (v.11). Binding these two incidents together is that tremendous statement we saw in verse 5: 'The Son of Man is Lord of the Sabbath.' This was an electrifying claim! After all, the sabbath was

instituted by God (Exodus 20:8-11); for Jesus to claim
authority over it could mean only one thing!

Lord of the harvest

Twelve ordinary men were now to play an important role
in the ministry of Jesus, both in terms of fellowship and
service (notice these in Mark 3:14,15). They were chosen
out of many disciples (the word means 'learners') to be
apostles (meaning 'special messengers'). But the really
instructive thing is to notice what Jesus did immediately
before he chose them (v.12). Now link this up with what
he said in Matthew 9:37,38. Prayer is not just *part* of our
responsibility in Christian service; it is the *first* part. We
need to pray for discernment, directions and the dynamic
of all we seek to do for the Lord of the harvest. In an age
of activism it is tempting to dash enthusiastically ahead
and then to pray for God's blessing on what we do. The
right approach is to get a grasp of the principles laid
down in John 15:5 and to pray *before* we act.

*'You call me "Teacher" and "Lord", and rightly so, for that is
what I am'* (John 13:13).

17

The sermon on the plain (1)

Luke 6:17-36

At this point in our studies in the biography of Jesus we
come to one of the occasions when Luke records for us
notes of a sermon which Jesus preached. It is sometimes

thought that this sermon is merely another version of what we call the Sermon on the Mount, which is recorded in Matthew 5, 6 and 7, but it is perhaps more likely that the sermon reported by Luke was given on a quite different occasion, though it did contain a number of similar sayings. One of the obvious differences in the two narratives is in the wording of the introductions to the sermons. Matthew says that Jesus 'went up on a mountainside' (Matthew 5:1), whereas Luke says that Jesus 'went down with them and stood on a level place' (v.17), though this could have been somewhere on a mountainside (see v.12). Needless to say, the context of the sermon in no way affects its content.

Life at its best

The sermon begins at verse 20 with a series of 'blessings' or, as we sometimes call them, 'beatitudes', changing at verse 24 to a series of 'woes'. Taken together, they form a collection of moral and spiritual bombshells, revolutionary concepts which challenged so many of the accepted teachings of the time. To summarize the first list, Jesus promised God's blessing on four groups of people: firstly, on those who did not trust in themselves (compare v.20 with Matthew 5:3 which brings out the meaning more clearly); secondly, on those who were spiritually hungry (compare v.21 with Matthew 5:6 which explains the kind of hunger Jesus meant); thirdly, on those who mourned over sin, and especially their own sin (compare v.21 with Matthew 5:4); and fourthly on those who suffered for the sake of their Christian faith and life (compare vv.22,23 with Matthew 5:10-12). In these few verses we are given God's blueprint for blessing. To what extent are you following the divine pattern? The 'woes' are addressed to the self-reliant, who go through life well off (v.24), well fed (v.25), well satisfied (v.25) and well thought of (v.26), and yet without a living faith in God (which is the inference we are meant to draw). Jesus was not suggesting that money, food, happiness and popularity were in any way wrong, but that they were *insufficient*. Although it is temporary, life must be seen in the light of eternity, and life at its best means putting God first, even when these apparently attractive things do not even come second! For the Christian, the guidelines are laid down in Colossians 3:1,2.

Love at its best

It would not be an over-simplification to say that Christian love is Christian faith in action, and Jesus now went on to take this love to its ultimate expression. The teaching of verses 27-36 could be summarized in one simple but stupendous phrase: 'Love your enemies' (vv.27,35). The Jews already knew the Old Testament command: 'Love your neighbour' (Leviticus 19:18), but many accepted the false corollary that they could therefore hate their enemies (Jesus quoted this in Matthew 5:43). Jesus now completely destroyed that false argument. As it is perfectly obvious that God pours out certain blessings even on those who openly disobey him, Christians should love their enemies and thus prove their own relationship to God (notice how this is put at vv.35,36). This particular section of the sermon is summed up in what is sometimes called 'the Golden Rule': 'Do to others as you would have them do to you' (v.31). To follow that rule will be to guarantee warm-hearted, generous, thoughtful, sacrificial kindness — and that is love at its best!

'Let us not love with words or tongue but with actions and in truth' (1 John 3:18).

─────────── **18** ───────────

The sermon on the plain (2)

Luke 6:37-49

The Jews had a word for a certain kind of preaching which we could literally translate as 'stringing beads together'. We have a good example of this in this particular passage, because in these thirteen verses, which can be read in about two minutes, Jesus touched on at least six different subjects.

Criticism

The promises contained in the three maxims Jesus lay down in verse 37 are true both on earth and in heaven. The man who is harsh and critical in his treatment of others will surely find those people behaving in exactly the same way towards him. But what is even more serious is that such an attitude on his part proves that he does not have the love of God in his heart. (By contrast notice what Paul says about the spiritual man in Romans 5:5.) And the man without the love of God in his heart is clearly not a Christian at all.

Generosity

In verse 38 we have another law which can be applied in two ways, practically and spiritually. On a human level, generosity tends to be contagious or at the least reciprocal — even among unconverted men! — as Jesus pointed out in verse 33. Beyond that, God promises

direct reward to those who are generous to others. Notice
how Paul puts this in Philippians 4:18,19!

Spiritual vision

Many of those who heard Jesus were not only learners,
they would one day be leaders. It was therefore vital
that they should know what they were teaching and
where they were going. Notice how Jesus applied this to
the Pharisees, comparing verses 39,40 with Matthew
15:12-14. It is surely stating the obvious to say that no
man can lead another to a place without first getting
there himself. Spiritually, this demands great discipline
and self-examination on the part of the Christian. James
3:1 warns of the presumption of thinking otherwise!

Hypocrisy

To illustrate this, Jesus uses the superb hyperbole of a
man with a plank of wood jutting out of his eye while he
tries to remove a tiny speck of sawdust from his brother's
eye (vv.41,42). It is easy to laugh at the picture, but not
so easy to obey the lesson it teaches. Before you criticize
others, be sure that you are not at fault in that area. If
you feel you must concern yourself with the failings of
others, make sure that you read Galatians 6:1 first!

Words and actions

The truths of verses 43,44 are obvious; and the application is equally plain, as Jesus pointed out in Matthew
7:15-20. A man's actions do not so much *make* his
character as *reveal* it — and so do his words! (v.45) Jesus
himself was a perfect example of this (look back at 4:22).
The exhortation in Hebrews 13:15 links fruit and speech
neatly together!

Obedience

The point of the well-known parable told in verses 46-49
is often missed. The foundation that Jesus commends is

not mere knowledge (both men had that — see vv.47,49) but *obedience*. It is only when we add the discipline of obedience (the building, digging and foundation-laying of v.48) to the raw materials of truth that we will have a structure that will stand the test of life. Obedience helps to build moral fibre; casual hearing gives a man no defence when trouble comes.

There is the further challenging truth that outward appearances can be deceptive. The fool's house would presumably look every bit as solid as the wise man's, but it failed the crucial test. Never be satisfied with shoddy building in your spiritual life. Make sure everything is built on solid rock.

'Do not merely listen to the word, and so deceive yourselves. Do what it says' (James 1:22).

19

'He healed the sick and raised the dead. . .'

Luke 7:1-17

'. . .Yes, he did!', the song goes on, and in today's reading we have an illustration of each of these remarkable miracles. From the detailed narratives, two features stand out vividly.

A soldier's faith
The centurion (v.1) was a high-ranking Roman soldier. From Luke's account of this particular incident, we can pull together some interesting threads of truth about his

character. For instance, we know that he was kind; although slaves were usually treated like pieces of furniture, this man had one 'whom his master valued highly' (v.2). Then, we know that he was tolerant. Jews and Gentiles usually mixed like mercury and water! (Notice what is said at John 4:9.) Yet the Jews were able to tell Jesus, 'This man. . .loves our nation' (vv.4,5). Next, the Jews made it clear that he was religiously inclined: not only had he shown an overall respect for them, but, in their own words, he had 'built our synagogue' (v.5). He was also remarkably humble: while his Jewish friends commended him to Jesus as deserving help, he took exactly the opposite line, and protested that he was not worthy either for Jesus to enter his house, nor that he himself should come near to Jesus (compare vv.6,7 with the attitude adopted by the tax-collector at Luke 18:13). But a further quality outshone even these — and that was his astonishing faith in the healing power of Jesus. He was apparently quite convinced that all Jesus had to do was to 'say the word' and the slave would recover (v.7). Jesus was so impressed with this that he ranked it as greater than any degree of faith he had ever found, even among the Jews (v.9). The centurion's reward matched his faith perfectly, for when the servants returned to the house they 'found the servant well' (v.10). This unnamed Roman soldier — perhaps not even a true disciple at this point — stands as a challenge to every Christian and as a rebuke to most. So many Christians badly need a faith lift! Defective faith results in aimlessness (Proverbs 3:5,6), uncertainty (2 Chronicles 20:20) and spiritual injury (Ephesians 6:16). The gift and the exercise of faith are absolutely essential for healthy growth in the Christian life. Notice where it fits with the picture of developing maturity at 2 Peter 1:5,6.

The Saviour's love

The next miracle took place just outside the Galilean town of Nain (v.11). Luke is the only New Testament writer to record the incident and he does so with artless simplicity and stunning effect. A widow's only son was being carried to the cemetery, accompanied by a large crowd of mourners (v.12). In what may have been very little more time than it takes to tell, Jesus comforted the widow (v.13), halted the procession and commanded the corpse to come back to life (v.14). With a perfect economy of words, Luke goes on, 'The dead man sat up and began to talk' (v.15). The reaction recorded in verses 16,17 is hardly surprising! There was little doubt in the minds of the people that they had seen God at work in their midst that day. Yet the loveliest thing in this incident is that we are told, 'When Jesus saw her, *his heart went out to her*' (v.13). His heart went out before either his hand or his word! The love of Jesus surges through the whole of the New Testament: John 13:1, Romans 8:35-39 and Galatians 2:20 are but a few examples. That our hearts should go out in love to him should surely be expected; that his should go out in love to us is amazing, and should have a decisive effect on our faith.

'I do believe; help me overcome my unbelief!' (Mark 9:24.)

20

Jesus and John

Luke 7:18-35

John the Baptist comes briefly back into the picture at
this stage. He was in prison at the time (the reason is
given in Matthew 14:3,4) but visiting friends had told
him about the astonishing things Jesus was doing (v.18).
The message he sent to Jesus leads us into today's
reading.

An anxious request
On the face of it, it seems strange that the question in
verses 19 and 20 should be asked by the one who had
confidently identified Jesus with the words: 'Look, the
Lamb of God, who takes away the sin of the world!'
(John 1:29.) Was he becoming impatient for Jesus to
take some political action to overthrow the Romans?
Was his faith beginning to fade? Was the question being
asked, not for John's own benefit, but on behalf of his
disciples? Was he wondering why Jesus did not mount
some spectacular rescue mission to get him out of prison?
Or were the reports he was getting so garbled that he
wanted more evidence? We are not told, but the very fact
that the question was asked is helpful to us. It shows that
in spite of the tremendous impact he made on his
generation John, like his great Old Testament counter-
part Elijah, was 'a man just like us' (James 5:17). He
knew what it was to be anxious, unsure and limited.

An ample reply

If lack of evidence prompted the question, Jesus quickly supplied the answer (v.22). Who could dispute the claims of a man who did these things? It tied in exactly with the prophecy by Isaiah that had been read by Jesus in the synagogue at Nazareth (look back to 4:18,19). In witness to others, learn to concentrate on the person and work of the Lord Jesus Christ. Winning philosophical, scientific or even religious arguments is no substitute for bringing people face to face with *him*. Notice how the other John brings out the importance of what Jesus did (John 2:11; 3:2; 7:31; 10:25,38; 20:30,31). Christianity is not based on philosophy, but on facts! Jesus then took the opportunity of commending John. He was not a fickle weakling (a reed swayed by the wind, v.24), nor an effeminate courtier ('a man dressed in fine clothes', v.25). Jesus identified him as a prophet who had been prophesied! (See Malachi 3:1; 4:5). What is more, he stood at the pinnacle of the prophets, the last (and in that sense the most important) of the line (v.28). Yet now, with the coming of Jesus, a new era had dawned and even the most insignificant Christian possessed greater privileges and blessings than John (v.28). Do you fully realize that? Have you begun to grasp what is meant by 1 Corinthians 3:21-23?

An angry rebuke

Jesus then turned from commending John to rebuking some of his hearers. Some acknowledged the truth of John's teaching and had in fact been baptized by him (v.29), but others had rejected both John and Jesus (v.30). They rejected John because they thought he was so austere that he must have been devil-possessed (v.33) and they rejected Jesus because they thought he was not austere enough (v.34). There was no pleasing them. They were like groups of fractious, restless children, unwilling to play either weddings or funerals (vv.31,32).

However, the changed lives of God's people prove the wisdom of his ways (v.35). Beware of criticizing other Christians just because they do things differently from you. There is room for great variety within the Christian church and God sometimes springs surprises! Remember that truth is often broader than man's traditions and that character is more important than life-style. Read John 21:20-22 and notice the last words!

'The Lord. . . loves those who pursue righteousness' (Proverbs 15:9).

21

The fruit of forgiveness

Luke 7:36-50

This incident took place at a dinner party in the house of a Pharisee by the name of Simon (vv.36,40). The theme of the story as Luke tells it is forgiveness and from his fascinating narrative three things stand out.

Forgiveness indicated
Mingling with the guests (perhaps on the fringe of the crowd) was a woman with a notorious reputation for living 'a sinful life' (v.37). But (so recently that the guests had not even heard of it?) something had happened to her. At one stage Jesus told his host, 'Her many sins *have been* forgiven' (v.47), and she must therefore have repented and changed her ways (notice the order of these words at 24:47). This may explain the boldness of her

actions. As the guests reclined at table (they would have
done this by leaning on one elbow, with their feet
stretched out behind them) she suddenly begun to weep.
As her tears fell on Jesus' feet, she knelt down, wiped
them with her hair and 'kissed them'. Then she anointed
his feet with perfume from an alabaster (and therefore
expensive) jar (vv.37,38). As we see later, this seemingly
extravagant demonstration of love was the result of her
deep sense of gratitude. The first part of verse 47 could
be paraphrased: 'She has shown this amount of love
because she has been forgiven so much sin.' Is your love
for Christ any indication of his love for you?

Forgiveness illustrated

When Simon saw what had happened, he thought that
Jesus did not realize who the woman was and that he
could not, therefore, be a prophet sent from God (v.39).
Although Simon had not said a word, we read that Jesus
'answered him' (v.40). He had not read Jesus' mind
correctly, but Jesus had read his! The story Jesus told
was perfectly straightforward (vv.41,42). One man owed
a certain money-lender 'five hundred denarii' (about
eighteen months' wages); another owed him 'fifty
denarii' (about two months' wages). As they were both
bankrupt, he cancelled both debts. We shall see the
application of the story in a moment, but notice that this
is a perfect illustration of forgiveness. It is a cancellation
of the debt incurred by disobedience. This is brought out
in Matthew's version of the Lord's prayer (Matthew
6:12). On the basis of 1 Chronicles 16:29, how often do
we need to be forgiven?

Forgiveness demonstrated

When Jesus asked Simon which of the two debtors would
love their benefactor the most, he quickly gave the right
answer (v.43). Jesus agreed, but then came the crunch!
Simon, as the host that evening, had not even performed

the common courtesies of the time towards him. He had
given him neither water to rinse his feet (see Genesis
18:4), the customary kiss of welcome (see Romans
16:16), nor the normal touch of perfumed oil on the head
(see Psalm 23:5). On the other hand, the uninvited
stranger had lavished tears, kisses and perfume on him.
The lesson was clear: much love was a sign of much
forgiveness and little love was a sign of little forgiveness
(v.47). Simon's actions (or lack of them) had betrayed
the state of his heart! To the amazement of the guests
(link v.49 with Luke 5:21), Jesus publicly announced her
forgiveness (v.48) and then commended her faith and
assured her that she could 'go in peace' (v.50).

The assurance of forgiveness is one of the greatest
blessings we can know in life; nothing else can bring such
peace of heart and mind. But Christians have a duty to
respond to this by holy living and faithful service. How
do you match up to what the apostle Paul says in 2
Corinthians 5:14,15?

'I love the Lord, for he heard my voice' (Psalm 116:1).

22

The purpose of the parables

Luke 8:1-15

A parable has been described as 'an earthly story with a
heavenly meaning'. Literally, the word means 'to put
things side by side in order to compare them'. In the
case of the parables of Jesus those two 'things' were a

short story and one particular spiritual truth, usually concerning the kingdom of God (look at what Jesus said in v.10). The New Testament contains nearly forty of the parables of Jesus and at one stage we even read that 'He did not say anything to them without using a parable' (Matthew 13:34). But if the parables of Jesus were so prominent, what was their purpose? There are two answers to that question, both of which can be seen in this particular passage.

To reveal the truth to some

Jesus made it clear that the meaning of this parable had to do with the way people listened to or received 'the word of God' (v.11). You can trace this in each part of his explanation of the story: he mentions 'the ones who hear' (v.12), 'the ones who receive the word' (v.13), 'those who hear' (v.14) and 'those. . . who hear the word' (v.15). In fact, when Jesus had told the parable to the crowds he added, 'He who has ears to hear, let him hear' (v.8). But notice what happened next. The disciples asked him what the parable meant (v.9). They were not satisfied with hearing a fascinating story and then indulging in idle speculation as to what it might mean. They wanted to *know* and they came to the Lord for the answer. That must always be our attitude when reading the Bible. We can never understand it by mere human reasoning. But the Christian has two priceless assets. One is the Holy Spirit, who, it is promised, will lead him to know the truth (notice what Jesus said in John 16:13). The other is prayer. Surely the words of James 1:5 apply here? Notice too how Jesus emphasized that spiritual understanding is a gift from God (see the beginning of v.10). Spiritual truths are 'mysteries' and only God can open them up to us. Get a grip on this and learn to be grateful when God enables you to 'see' what the Bible means. Matthew 11:25 will help to keep your gratitude humble!

To conceal the truth from others
However harsh this may seem, we must not run away
from this very important point. Notice how it is made in
the parable itself. People who hear the word casually,
carelessly or superficially are like seed falling on a well-
trodden path (compare v.5 with v.12), or on 'rock'
(compare v.6 with v.13), or among 'thorns' (compare v.7
with v.14) — all failing to come to fruition. The whole
point is devastatingly crystallized in the second part of
verse 10 (compare Psalm 78:2; Isaiah 6:9,10). Those who
treat parables as no more than interesting stories will end
up with nothing but interesting stories! In spiritual
matters the clarity of men's hearing depends on the state
of their hearts. Elsewhere Jesus went even further and
said that a man must be willing to *do* God's will before he
will be able to *discern* it (see John 7:17). The man who is
not prepared to *heed* the Word of God will not even be
able to *hear* it correctly! It is for this reason that the
parables become *windows* to some people and *walls* to
others. Learn to come to the Bible fulfilling all the
conditions mentioned in verse 15. Galatians 5:22,23 is a
sample of the kind of harvest that can be expected!

'If you call out for insight. . . then you will understand'
(Proverbs 2:3-5).

23

Living the Christian life

Luke 8:16-25

Not for the first time, our day's reading covers several apparently unconnected paragraphs, in this case three of them. Even if they were totally unrelated, they would not, of course, lose any of their authority, as they would still be part of God's Word. Taken together, however, they focus attention on three facets of living the Christian life.

Responsibility

The command to 'consider carefully how you listen' links the first paragraph (vv.16-18) with the parable of the sower (look back at v.8) and reminds us of the responsibility of being an attentive *hearer* of God's Word. But we are also to be *doers* and 'not merely listen to the word' (James 1:22), and the two are vitally connected! Seed will bear fruit and a candle will light up a room *if put in the right place*; the psalmist tells us of one very important responsibility in this area (Psalm 119:11). But there is another sense in which it must never be hidden (v.16). Jesus makes our responsibility even more solemn by reminding us that at the end of the day secrecy is impossible (link v.17 with 2 Corinthians 5:10). To all of this Jesus added a word of encouragement and a word of warning (v.18). One of God's spiritual laws could be summed up in the words: 'use or lose' (see the parable of the talents, for instance, in Matthew 25:14-30, and especially the last two verses).

Obedience

The themes of hearing and obeying God's Word are repeated yet again at the end of this incident (vv.19-21). The people who made the very ordinary comment in verse 20 could hardly have expected the reply they received (v.21), which incidentally contains one of the Bible's loveliest descriptions of the relationship between Christians and the Lord Jesus. True believers are not seen by Jesus as mere slaves, but as friends (see John 15:15) and, even closer than that, as members of his family. If you look up Romans 8:17 you will see that this has relevance for the future as well as for the present! But notice, by linking verse 21 with John 15:14 and 1 John 3:14, how the reality of that relationship can be tested. Are you developing the family likeness and deepening the family love? These are the marks of *true* Christianity (see John 13:35).

Faith

Weary after his long exertions, Jesus obviously wanted to cross the Sea of Galilee for a break from the demanding crowds. As he slept, a sudden storm swept down from the hills (v.23). Galilee is over 600 feet below sea level and cool evening air rushing down the ravines in the hills produces exactly this result. Frightened out of their wits and believing that they were going to be drowned, the disciples cried to Jesus for help (v.24). Waking up, he rebuked the wind and the waves and in an instant the storm was over (v.24). On a previous occasion Jesus had 'rebuked' the fever gripping Peter's mother-in-law (see 4:39). Disease in the body and disorder in the natural world are ultimately (but not always directly) the result of sin's entry into the world and these two incidents are vivid demonstrations of Christ's authority in both

spheres! Finally, there was a rebuke (though of a
different kind) for the disciples: 'Where is your faith?'
(v.25) They had been so frightened by the power of the
wind that they had forgotten the greater power of the
Lord. The Christian life is certainly not without its
storms, but the Christian is never without a Saviour at
hand to help and when he does so stillness takes their
place. No crisis is greater than Christ! Incidentally the
answer to the disciples' question in verse 25 is found in
Psalm 89:8,9!

'Submit. . . to God. . . resist the devil' (James 4:7).

24

The divine Exorcist

Luke 8:26-40

There is world-wide interest in the activities of evil spirits
and a great deal of discussion on how they can be dealt
with. This passage shows us that neither the problem nor
the solution are in any way new. In today's study we
shall basically look at three phases of a remarkable
incident which Luke describes.

Diagnosis

As Jesus stepped ashore he was met by a man in a
desperate condition. He was demon-possessed, naked
and lived among the dead in the local cemetery (v.27).
Luke not only identifies an 'evil spirit' (v.29), but 'many
demons' (v.30) who had taken possession of the man. Yet

perhaps nothing gives clearer evidence of the supernatural power of evil spirits than the diagnosis *they* made!
(Compare v.28 with Matthew 8:29; Mark 5:7.) No mere
madman would have that kind of knowledge. It is
staggering to realize that evil spirits recognized Jesus
when most of the people did not, and that they did so
long before even someone like Peter made his great
declaration of faith (see 9:20). In that sense, faith is not
confined to Christians, nor even to men at large (see
James 2:19). Never underestimate the reality or the
ability of what Paul calls 'the powers of this dark world'
(Ephesians 6:12). Our attitude in this particular area is
laid down for us very clearly in Deuteronomy 18:10-14.

Direction
All attempts at taming this frightening, wild man had
failed (v.29). There was no natural solution to a supernatural problem. The evil spirits instantly recognized
that in Jesus they were faced with one who had authority
over them. Notice that they pleaded with him not to
order them 'to go into the Abyss' (v.31). This is a
reference to the bottomless pit to which Satan and all his
hosts will eventually be condemned (see Revelation 9:1;
11:7; 20:1-15). Instead, they asked to be allowed to enter
a herd of swine (v.32), possibly in a frantic attempt to
stave off or delay their inevitable doom. Given permission, they entered the pigs (there were about 2,000
of them — see Mark 5:13), at which 'the herd rushed
down the steep bank into the lake and was drowned'
(v.33). Why did Jesus allow this loss of livestock? The
best answer would seem to be that he did so to help the
man to *see* that his terrible ordeal was over. One man's
health and sanity were more important than the lives of
2,000 animals. Man has been given God's authority to
kill animals to supply his need for food; surely the Lord
had authority to use them to supply a man's need of
faith? But the key point here is that the only ultimate

answer to demon possession was demon expulsion, and
what was true then was true in the New Testament after
Jesus' ascension (see Acts 8:7, for instance) and remains
true today.

Deliverance

The effect on the man was remarkable. People who came
to see what had happened found him 'dressed and in his
right mind' (v.35). Rid of the evil spirits, he was socially,
morally and mentally reintegrated. All of this is in turn a
picture of the truth that Jesus makes men 'whole'; the
Bible says that it is only 'in Christ' that men are given
'fulness' (Colossians 2:10). When the healed man asked
if he might travel with him, Jesus refused his request and
instead commanded him to return to his own neighbours
and tell them what God had done for him (v.39). What
extraordinary grace this showed! The people wanted to
get rid of Jesus and he condescended to leave, but not
before appointing a missionary to share the gospel with
them. Are you seriously seeking to bear a testimony to
Christ in the situation in which God has placed you?

'My mouth will speak in praise of the Lord' (Psalm 145:21).

25

Faith works!

Luke 8:41-56

Today's reading weaves together incidents concerning
two very different people who both experienced the

miraculous, healing touch of the Lord Jesus Christ; what
links the two stories together is the great faith of the
people involved in them.

Dying. . .

The passage opens with a man called Jairus coming to
Jesus in great distress because his twelve-year-old
daughter lay dying (vv.41,42). Although he was 'a ruler
of the synagogue' and therefore a leading figure in the
religious community, notice that in his hour of need he
'fell at Jesus' feet' (v.41). Real faith always goes hand in
hand with genuine humility. The Bible gives a solemn
warning and a wonderful promise when it says that
'God opposes the proud but gives grace to the humble'
(1 Peter 5:5). Whenever you begin to feel self-sufficient,
you will cease to ask God for his help and when you cease
to ask you cease to receive (check this with the end of
James 4:2). In the case of Jairus, humility was married to
extraordinary faith: Mark tells us that he asked Jesus,
'Please come and put your hands on her so that she will
be healed and live' (Mark 5:23).

. . . Dying. . .

As Jesus started out for the home of Jairus, a woman who
had been suffering from an incurable haemorrhage for
twelve years 'touched the edge of his cloak' (v.44). As we
are told elsewhere, she was convinced that 'If I just touch
his clothes, I will be healed' (Mark 5:28). This showed
amazing faith, in that no similar thing is recorded as having happened before! Her faith was rewarded instantly
(v.44), but it brought a puzzling question from Jesus
(v.45). When Peter pointed out that many people had
been pressing against him (v.45), Jesus insisted that
following one person's touch power had gone out of him
(v.46). Realizing that she could not escape attention, the
woman, although terrified, owned up (v.47). She was
immediately comforted by Jesus with the words: 'Your

faith has healed you' (v.48). But why did Jesus insist on identifying her? According to laws laid down in the Old Testament (see Leviticus 15:25-30), a woman in her condition was ceremonially unclean and contaminated anyone she touched. It was therefore very important that everyone should know of her cure, so that she could return to normal life. What marvellous understanding Jesus showed, and what a reminder to us that though sometimes hard, obedience is always rewarded! (See Exodus 19:5.)

. . . Dead!

While this was happening, Jairus' daughter had died and her father's request now seemed pointless (v.49). Yet Jesus told him that he must still have faith; his daughter would be restored (v.50). Arriving at the house he found it already filled with the usual professional mourning-party (including musicians, see Matthew 9:23). When he told them to stop wailing, because the girl was only asleep, they 'laughed at him' because they knew perfectly well that she was dead (v.53). But Jesus was using the same kind of language as he did concerning Lazarus (see John 11:11-14). The reality of her death is shown by the words describing the miracle that followed: 'Her spirit returned' (v.55). The lovely touch at the end of verse 55 reminds us that Jesus is as concerned about the ordinary provision of meals as the extraordinary performance of miracles! Matthew 6:25-34 gives beautiful confirmation of this and is in turn a direct challenge to exercise daily faith in God for the provision of the little as well as the large things of life. Our God is God of the mundane as well as the miraculous.

'Have faith in God' (Mark 11:22).

26

Enough for every need

Luke 9:1-17

As with yesterday's reading, we have two separate
incidents here, linked by one common feature — in this
case the Lord's ability to supply all people's needs,
whatever their circumstances.

The sending of the messengers

The first thing mentioned in this chapter needs to be seen
in the light of the fact that the life of Jesus was
approaching a critical phase. His ministry in Galilee
would soon be over (look ahead to what is said in v.51)
and popularity would soon be replaced by opposition.
Jesus therefore made specific plans to send the disciples
out to make a final concentrated effort in the area (v.1).
Although Luke does not mention the fact, it is interesting
to notice that they went out in six teams of two (see Mark
6:7). Luke does, however, tell us three very important
things about the ministry of these men. Firstly, it was a
delegated ministry. The 'power and authority' they had
was not their own (v.1), nor was the kingdom they were
to preach! (v.2) In all your Christian work, remember
who is the Lord and who are the labourers (see 10:2).
Then it was a *definite* ministry. They were to 'preach
the kingdom of God and. . . heal the sick' (v.2).
Their business was not political propaganda nor moral
platitudes. Instead, they were to minister in God's name

to men's spiritual and physical needs. The miracles
would have underlined their doctrine in a most powerful
way. Finally, it was a *dependent* ministry. Look at verse 3.
The 'bag' may have been the equivalent of a begging-
bowl, which was used by some itinerant preachers at that
time. But whatever the precise detail, the principle was
clear: they were to travel light, depending on God to
provide food, shelter and clothing as they were needed. It
all sounds pretty hazardous, but you can check at 22:35
as to whether it worked out! God never calls a man to do
a work for him without guaranteeing his lines of supply
and sometimes he asks a man to start with no resources
in sight. But this is not always the case (see 22:36).

The feeding of the multitude

This is one of the best-known stories in the New
Testament, recorded in all four Gospels. When they
returned from their extraordinary mission, Jesus held a
debriefing session with the disciples and then took them
by boat (see Mark 6:32) for rest and relaxation (v.10).
Time spent quietly alone with Jesus is never time wasted.
But soon they were thronged again (compare v.11 with
Mark 6:33,34) and Jesus immediately began preaching
and healing those who were sick (v.11). As evening drew
on, the disciples asked him to send the people away for
food and lodging (v.12). When Jesus (with a smile?)
suggested that they feed them, the disciples replied that
there was hardly any food available — just five loaves
and two fish belonging to a small boy (compare v.15 with
John 6:8,9). Although there were over 5,000 people in the
crowd (read v.14 with Matthew 14:21) Jesus ordered
them to sit down in groups of fifty (vv.14,15). He then
'gave thanks' (v.16) and asked the disciples to begin
passing the food to the people. Amazingly, it never ran
out; everybody had enough to eat and even the crumbs
filled twelve baskets (v.17). There have been attempts to
explain away this miracle, but in the light of Psalm 33:6

and John 1:3 this is totally unnecessary! Notice the link
between all of this and our studies yesterday on the
subject of faith. Finally, read David's testimony in Psalm
37:25. Do you think the same holds true today? If so, how
should this affect your approach to life?

'My God will meet all your needs' (Philippians 4:19).

27

The cross and the crown

Luke 9:18-36

As we saw yesterday, our studies have reached a turning-
point in the earthly life of Jesus. He now felt that it was
time to assess the response to his ministry. The question
in verse 18 brought an extraordinary answer (v.19).
Many people thought that Jesus was a reincarnation of
John the Baptist; others thought that he was the prophet
Elijah (with whose teaching that of John the Baptist had
already been linked — see 1:17); while others thought
that he was another of the prophets come back to life.
Jesus immediately made it clear that the issue must be
taken further; the inescapable question was 'Who do *you*
say I am?' (v.20) Christianity is concerned with the
person of Christ as well as with his works and it demands
an individual response, not merely knowledge of other
people's opinions. Peter's answer (compare v.20 with the
fuller rendering in Matthew 16:16) marks one of the most
electrifying moments in the New Testament. 'Christ' is
the equivalent of 'Messiah', the promised Deliverer for

whom the Jews were longing. To avoid the impression that as Messiah he would spark off a revolt against the Roman occupying forces, Jesus gave strict instructions to the disciples not to break the astonishing news (v.21). Bringing in the kingdom of God was to involve other things, both for Christ and for Christians.

The way for Christ

Far from leading a triumphant popular uprising, Jesus went on to say that as Messiah he would be rejected and killed (v.22). The Old Testament prophets had certainly forecast this (read Isaiah 53:12 for instance); now Jesus confirmed their words. About a week later (v.28) during an extraordinary meeting with Moses and Elijah, the only topic of conversation mentioned is his death (v.31). Jesus was under no illusions about the cost involved in redeeming the world. But while his death was a tragedy, it was not an accident. It had all been foretold (look ahead to 22:37). Yet the cross was not to be the end of the story. Firstly, Jesus said that he would rise from the dead after three days (v.22); then, he spoke of returning to earth in triumphant glory (v.26); finally, he heard the Father's voice of loving assurance when he was transfigured on the mountain-top (v.35). Jesus knew that there was a crown beyond the cross. Make a careful note of the significance of this in Hebrews 12:2!

The way for Christians

The passage also tells us that Christians have a parallel (though not identical) experience. The Christian must 'take up his cross' (v.23), that is to say, he must die to all his own self-centred desires, ambitions and aims. What is more, he must do it 'daily'. Christian living is not a matter of fits and starts, but rather of continuous discipline and dedication. Emphasizing the point, Jesus said that the Christian must 'lose his life', abandoning self-satisfaction as a philosophy. But such living brings

its reward. Notice how this comes across in the passage.
Firstly, Jesus said that the person who lost his life in this
way would 'save it' (v.24). Then, the appearance of
Moses and Elijah would have been a great encouragement to Peter, James and John, and an assurance to
them of a life of glory beyond the grave. Notice that when
Peter referred to it later, it was immediately after a
reference to his own death (2 Peter 1:13-18). To bear the
cross is to prepare for the crown! The way for Christians
is one of discipline, determination and self-crucifixion,
but there is a powerful motive to draw us on. The apostle
Paul tells us about it in Philippians 3:12-14.

*'We share in his sufferings in order that we may also share in his
glory'* (Romans 8:17).

28

Disappointing disciples
and others

Luke 9:37-62

Today's rather longer reading gathers up five incidents
which can help us to learn from the failings of the people
they describe. Like the rest of the Bible, these verses were
'written to teach us' (Romans 15:4). The five incidents
point out at least four flaws in the people concerned.

Unbelief
When Jesus came down from the mountain he was
immediately surrounded by a crowd (v.37). One
man was in terrible distress because his son was

demon-possessed and suffering from screaming fits and
convulsions (v.39). He had asked the disciples to heal
him, but they had not been able to do so (v.40). Even as
they were speaking, the boy was thrown to the ground by
the evil spirit (v.42). Jesus immediately rebuked the evil
spirit, healed the boy and tenderly restored him to his
father (v.42). But notice the rebuke in verse 41. Perhaps
the crowd in general is included in this, but Matthew
17:19,20 seems to indicate those who were especially
guilty! As we can see from verses 43-45, they were not
even clear yet about how Jesus was to fulfil his mission.
In spite of all they had seen Jesus do and of the power
they had been given (check this back at v.1) they were
still weakened by unbelief. For the world at large, this
was predictable because predicted (see John 12:37,38),
but it was a great tragedy for disciples of Christ. Are you
living at the level of God's promises? How do you react,
for instance, to 2 Corinthians 1:20 and 7:1?

Pride

Coming so soon after what Jesus said in verse 44, the
words of verse 46 are shocking. Were some of them
jealous of Peter, James and John? Knowing what was in
their minds, Jesus used a child as a visual aid (v.47). He
taught them that to render lowly service in his name was
to serve him and that true humility had its own reward
(v.48). Beware of pride in any part of your Christian life
and service. In the light of Matthew 5:48 such a thing is
both ignorant and sinful!

Intolerance

There are two incidents in verses 49-56. In the first, the
disciples reported that they had put a stop to a man
casting out devils in Christ's name because he was not
a member of their group. Were they jealous of his
success? (Link v.49 with v.40.) Perhaps they expected
to be commended; instead, Jesus corrected them and

told them, 'Whoever is not against you is for you' (v.50). Joshua had made a similar mistake (see Numbers 11:24-30). Beware of negatively criticizing those seeking to do God's work without toeing your particular party line. In the second incident, the disciples wanted God to incinerate the Samaritans who openly rejected Jesus! In reply, he said that that kind of spirit was wholly alien to Christians (v.55). His own purpose in coming into the world pointed the right way (v.56). Notice how the Bible says we are to deal with those who oppose the Christian message (2 Timothy 2:24-26).

Half-heartedness

In verses 57-62 three unknown people flirt briefly with the idea of becoming Christians. The first sounded full of enthusiasm (v.57), but had failed to count the cost (v.58). The second wanted to wait until his father had died (v.59); but that might have been years away and the kingdom of God made a more urgent claim (v.60). The third made a seemingly innocent request (v.61), but Jesus detected a weakness and insisted that a Christian must keep his eyes firmly fixed in one direction (v.62). Contrast these people with the instructions given in 1 Peter 1:13 and think carefully where you stand!

'Caleb. . . followed the Lord wholeheartedly' (Deuteronomy 1:36).

29

Ambassadors for Christ

Luke 10:1-24

These verses record the sending out by Jesus of a second wave of evangelistic commandos. Manuscripts differ as to whether there were seventy or seventy-two (v.1), but much more important were the context and nature of their ministry. Three words will help us to capture some of the truth in this passage.

Responsibility

Their mission was one involving great *danger*; they would be like lambs among wolves (v.3). It was to be made in great *dependence*; much the same as the twelve sent out earlier, they were to take neither 'purse or bag or [spare?] sandals' (v.4). And it was to be a mission involving great *dedication*; they were not to waste time in idle chatter (compare v.4 with 2 Kings 4:29), in quibbling over ceremonial food regulations (v.7) or in endless social activities (v.7). Their mission was urgent and important. By divine appointment (v.1) they were involved in nothing less than 'the kingdom of God' (v.9) and when they spoke they would do so in the Lord's name (see v.16). As with the previous group, they were authorized and empowered to heal and to preach (v.9), but notice another responsibility (v.2). We need constantly to examine ourselves in all of these areas. As ambassadors for Christ (see 2 Corinthians 5:20) we are under a solemn obligation to fulfil our God-given mandate. We may not be what we call 'full-time', but we must be whole-hearted. In passing, notice that a great responsibility also rested on those who heard their preaching (vv.10-15). Sodom, Tyre and Sidon had all come under the judgement of God because of their sin; the fate of those who rejected the clear preaching of the gospel would be even worse. To realize that will surely make us more determined than ever to preach the gospel faithfully and plainly.

Revelation

The fact that these messengers were appointed by the Lord can now be linked to words he spoke to his Father (vv.21,22) and to them on their return (vv.23,24). In the first two verses we are told that Christianity is not a matter of human research or reasoning, but of divine revelation. 'These things' would refer to the general body of truth Jesus had taught the disciples; but the crucial truth centred around the related identities of God the Father and God the Son. Only Jesus could reveal this to men. This is a fundamental biblical truth; take time to read 1 Corinthians 2:9-14 and 2 Corinthians 4:3-6 very carefully and notice how this all fits into the context of evangelism. In verses 23,24 we are told that the first disciples were given the added privilege of a physical revelation. Generations of Jews had longed for the Messiah; these men were actually seeing him. No wonder Jesus called them 'blessed' (v.23). We too should rejoice at all that the Lord has been pleased to reveal to us in his Word.

Rejoicing

When the disciples returned from their mission, they gave an excited report about the success of it all (v.17). In reply, Jesus said three things. Firstly, he said that he had seen Satan himself fall from heaven (v.18). He may have said this in order to put their triumphs in perspective or to warn them against the danger of pride, which caused Satan's downfall (1 Timothy 3:6). Secondly, he reminded them that the authority and power they had was not self-generated; it had been given to them by him (v.19). Thirdly, he taught that a man's main cause for rejoicing should not be his Christian service, but his Christian status (v.20). Knowing how prone men are to concentrate on what God does *through* them (and their tendency to claim some of the credit!) Jesus skilfully turned the disciples' attention to what God had done *to* them, entirely without their help. When a person has reason to believe that his name is written in 'the book of life' (Philippians 4:3) then he has reason, not to boast (for it is none of his doing), but to rejoice.

'Come. . . take your inheritance, the kingdom prepared for you' (Matthew 25:34).

———————— **30** ————————

A day of questions

Luke 10:25-42

Today's reading includes what may be the best-known story in the Bible, the parable of the Good Samaritan. It is also one of the most misused and subject to interpretations that are sometimes fascinating but often false. We can keep to the real meaning of the story by taking careful note of the questions that surround it.

Question 1

The first question was asked by 'an expert' in Old
Testament law, no doubt specializing in the law of
Moses, contained in the first five books. His first
question was deliberately asked 'to test Jesus' (v.25). He
wanted to know how this wandering Galilean preacher
would answer an important question very much in
people's minds at the time (compare 18:18).

Questions 2 and 3

In return, Jesus asked two parallel questions which
pinned the man down to his specialist subject, 'the Law'
(v.26). The man's reply showed a very clear grasp of
the Old Testament, for in quoting from Deuteronomy
6:5 and Leviticus 19:18 he was crystallizing the Ten
Commandments, just as Jesus did in Mark 12:29-31.
Now in theory he was right; the man who kept the
law perfectly would 'live' (v.28). But as no man had
ever done so, gaining eternal life by keeping the law
was a purely hypothetical notion. The law's real
intention was quite different (see Romans 3:20;
Galatians 3:23,24). However, Jesus took the man up on
his answer and said, '*Do this* and you will live' (v.28).
Realizing that he was now trapped into admitting his
own failure (and therefore the insincerity of his first
question) the lawyer tried to justify himself by raising a
point of interpretation.

Question 4

According to their traditional teaching, the Jews were
under no obligation to love those outside of their own
race and religion. These people were not their 'neighbours'. If Jesus confirmed this line of thought, the man
would be off the hook! So the lawer asked, 'And who is
my neighbour?' (v.29) In reply, Jesus told a story. A man
travelling on the notorious Jericho Road was beaten,
robbed and left for dead (v.30). Some time later a priest

came along, took one look at him and hurried on (v.31).
Then a Levite (another religious official) came along and
did likewise (v.32). Notice that these two not only left the
dying man there; they 'passed by on the other side'
(vv.31,32). Presumably they thought he was dead and
did not want to become ceremonially unclean by
touching a dead body (see Numbers 19:11). Then a
Samaritan came along. Seeing the wounded man, he
rushed to give him first aid, took him to an inn and
agreed to pay for his entire convalescence! (vv.33-35)
The people would have been stunned by this, as the Jews
and the Samaritans were constantly at loggerheads (see
John 4:9).

Question 5

The lawyer had asked a question about *identifying* a
neighbour; Jesus now asked a question about *being* one
(v.36). The answer was obvious and the implication
inescapable (v.37). However else this story is used, its
real purpose is to show that *everyone* is our 'neighbour'
and that we are to give whatever help we can to those we
find in need, regardless of race, rank, colour, creed or
anything else. To think this through is to realize that
here is the very heart of practical Christianity.

In closing this section, Luke inserts an incident at
Bethany (vv.38-42). The narrative speaks for itself.
Perhaps Luke put it in alongside the story of the Good
Samaritan to balance the lawyer's preoccupation with
the 'second commandment'. Only the Christian pre-
pared to sit at the feet of Jesus will be able to stand in the
face of the world! Worship comes before service and the
King before the King's business (see Matthew 4:10).

'Worship the Lord in the splendour of his holiness' (Psalm 96:9).

31

How to pray

Luke 11:1-13

Every Christian should identify with the disciples when
they asked Jesus to meet one of man's greatest spiritual
needs ('Lord, teach us to pray' (v.1)) and should be
profoundly grateful that the New Testament preserves
for all time the answer he gave. His reply covers thirteen
verses in Luke's account and for study purposes can
usefully be divided into three parts.

The pattern he gave
The words of verses 2-4, together with the version in
Matthew 6:9-13, are probably the best known in the
whole Bible. We usually call them 'The Lord's prayer',
though we can be sure there was at least one part of it
that Jesus never used at all (link the beginning of v.4
with Hebrews 4:15 for the explanation). The opening
words of verse 2 show that Jesus meant us to use this
prayer as it is (compare Matthew 6:9). The Jews were
quite familiar with set, formal prayers and rabbis often
taught them to their followers (notice the end of v.1
where John is said to have done the same thing). But it is
also a model for *all* prayer, in three ways: *Firstly,* because
of what it says about *God*. It puts God first; (notice the
first three petitions in verse 2). Prayer is not meant to be
a selfish shopping-list. Our first concern should be for
God's glory (see Deuteronomy 26:2; Matthew 6:33).

Secondly, because of what it says about *man;* as verse 3
shows, man is utterly dependent on God's goodness and
provision, even for his physical survival (so much for the
devil's lie in Genesis 3:5!). *Thirdly,* because of what it
says about *sin;* the three final petitions are all about the
same subject, which obviously infers that holiness of life
should be the Christian's constant concern (check 1
Thessalonians 4:3, where its importance is put in the
simplest possible terms).

The parable he told
The story in verses 5-10 is not without humour! In a tiny
Jewish home there would normally be just one room and
the family would sleep on the floor, huddled together for
warmth in a raised part farthest from the door. The split-
level design would allow for the domestic animals to
sleep in the same room, but on the lower level, nearest
the door. For the man of the house to open the door to a
midnight caller would almost certainly mean disturbing
the sleeping children (v.7) — to say nothing of causing
chaos among the chickens! But in the story the visitor
refused to give in, so the man had to get up! There are
probably two lessons here. One is the need to persist in
prayer; 'persistence' in verse 8 literally means 'shame-
lessness'! Jesus was to devote a whole parable to this
later on (see Luke 18:1-8, and especially v.1, which gives
the reason for that parable). But the primary lesson of
the parable told here was underlined in another way.

The principle he established
The key phrase in verses 11-13 is 'How much more will
your Father in heaven. . . ?' (v.13). Notice now how the
whole passage slots together. The questions in verses
11-12 are about *fathers,* who, for all their human
sinfulness, give good things to their children (v.13); the
householder in the parable is a *father,* but also a friend
(see v.5), who, even if reluctantly, will not leave his

friend in need; and at the beginning of the Lord's prayer, Christians are encouraged to address God as *'Father'* (v.2)! God is not a miser, reluctant to give; on the contrary, he longs to pour out blessing on his children, for whom there is no greater gift than the Holy Spirit (see v.13 and compare with Psalm 84:11). The whole of this record could be summed up in this way: the *pattern* tells us that we should pray inclusively; the *parable* tells us that we should pray persistently; the *principle* tells us that we should pray expectantly!

'If any of you lacks. . . he should ask God, who gives generously to all' (James 1:5).

32

Jesus — Deity or devil?

Luke 11:14-36

Throughout his public ministry, Jesus was the centre of controversy (see John 7:43, for instance) — a fact which carries with it the incidental lesson that even at our best we will not always meet with approval. Here, as elsewhere, his very nature was being questioned. It will help us in our study if we divide this somewhat longer passage into five sections.

Accusation
When Jesus restored a man's speech by casting out a spirit of dumbness, 'the crowd was amazed' (v.14). But some people flatly accused him of using satanic power

('Beelzebub', in v.15, was probably a corruption of the name of a heathen Philistine god — see 2 Kings 1:2 — and was commonly used as a Jewish synonym for the devil). However, not everybody agreed with such an appalling assessment; instead, they asked Jesus to give them some kind of supernatural indication that the source of his power lay elsewhere (v.16).

Argument
Jesus began his reply with cool and unanswerable logic. Surely evil set against evil could only mean self-destruction? (v.17) Was Satan out to defeat himself? (v.18) And what about other Jews who had cast out devils — were they also in league with the devil? (v.19) There is a fine and important lesson in all of this cut and thrust: while we are never to be argumentative (see 2 Timothy 2:23-25) we must not be afraid of using strong, forceful argument (compare Paul's example at Acts 19:8). Christian witness involves hard, careful thinking, not just throwing clumps of texts at people!

Attestation
So far the kind of argument Jesus was using inferred that he was using divine power; now he said so plainly (v.20). The devil is 'strong' (v.21), but God is 'stronger' (v.22) and when he attacks, Satan's defences are powerless. This was exactly what Jesus had been doing; what more attestation could they need? It is interesting to link together John 14:11 and 3:2!

Application
Notice that this is no idle theorizing; it has many practical applications. In the first place, there can be no neutrality on the question of who Jesus is (v.23). Nobody can sit on the fence here; a man must make up his mind (compare 1 Kings 18:21). Then, being a Christian does not just mean agreeing to an occasional spring-clean; it

means the discipline of a continuing moral revolution (vv.24-26). Only God can bring about the desire for that change and the change itself. Only the Holy Spirit can banish evil spirits. Thirdly, those who reject the clear evidence Christ gave will be condemned (vv.29-32). As we saw, some Jews had asked Jesus for 'a sign' (v.16), but the only one he would give them was one they did not want — his own resurrection! (See Matthew 12:40 for the link with Jonah.) The heathen Ninevites had repented when Jonah preached to them (Jonah 3:5), and Jesus was greater than Jonah (v.32); the Queen of Sheba had been convinced by the wisdom of Solomon (1 Kings 10:4-9), and Jesus was greater than Solomon (v.31). The Jews were without excuse. Finally, just as a man must be clear-eyed to walk safely (v.34), so he must be clear-minded on spiritual issues if his life is to be 'completely lighted' (v.36).

Adoration

Yet in the midst of all the disbelief, doubt and downright opposition, at least one voice was raised in recognition and adoration (v.27). Jesus replied to this inspired exclamation with a reminder that knowledge demands obedience (v.28). The New Testament knows no other kind of Christianity (see Revelation 22:14). Are you living up to the light you have?

'Ascribe to the Lord the glory due to his name' (1 Chronicles 16:29).

33

Beware the woes of Jesus!

Luke 11:37-54

It all began with a dinner-party (v.37), but before he left
the house in which the meal was held Jesus had revealed
the terrible spiritual condition of many of the guests. Six
times in this passage he uses the exclamation 'Woe!'
Although not a word of final judgement, it does contain a
serious warning. Be prepared to expose your own life to
the light of God's Word as we examine what Jesus found
in these people.

Law instead of love

The discussion was sparked off when Jesus failed to wash
his hands before eating (v.38). (The hand-washing
referred to was a fantastic ceremonial rigmarole and had
nothing to do with hygiene.) In reply to his host's
amazement, Jesus pronounced his first 'Woe!' (v.42) —
on those who paid meticulous attention to ceremonial
and traditional details of the law (see vv.39,42) but were
inwardly 'full of greed and wickedness' (v.39). They were
more concerned with man-made laws than with 'the love
of God' (v.42).

Pomp instead of piety

For many of the Pharisees, church-going was no more
than an opportunity to display themselves. The 'most
important seats in the synagogues' (v.43) were in full

public view and were reserved for distinguished guests.
The Pharisees made sure that they were never empty!
But no man can exalt himself and God at the same time.
Isaiah 42:8 and John 3:30 are worth reading in this
connection!

Hindrance instead of help

Jewish graves were usually well marked with some kind
of whitewash so that people would know exactly where
they were, as any contact with a grave could cause the
person concerned to become ceremonially defiled. Jesus
now accused some of the Pharisees of being like
'unmarked graves'. As religious leaders, they should
have been a help to others, but by their actions and
attitudes they were often a positive hindrance to those
who came into contact with them. Take another look
back at verse 23. Is your life, taken as a whole, likely to
draw people to Christ or drive them from him?

Preaching insteads of practising

The 'experts in the law' were Old Testament students,
closely linked to the Pharisees. One of them now
protested that Jesus was tarring all of them with the
same brush (v.45). In reply, Jesus singled them out for
special criticism! For example, they insisted on people
keeping all the fantastic details of their man-made
religious laws, while they themselves found ways of
avoiding them (v.46). Notice Paul's words about this in
Romans 2:17-23. The Christian should always practise
what he preaches, and not just because actions speak
louder than words.

Ritual instead of repentance

By Hebrew chronology, Abel (Genesis 4:8) and
Zechariah (2 Chronicles 24:20,21) were the first and last
Old Testament martyrs. By elaborate attention to the
tombs of martyred prophets (v.47) the lawyers tried to

exempt themselves from guilt (see Matthew 23:30). But
their ritualistic sorrow was sheer hypocrisy — after all,
they were planning to kill the greatest Prophet of all! (See
vv.53,54.) No wonder Jesus said what he did in verse 50.

Ignorance instead of insight
Though they were Bible students, they had so perverted
and complicated the Scriptures that they had missed
their saving message and even confused people on the
brink of grasping it (v.52). What a solemn challenge to
us to submit to the plain teaching of Scripture and to be
crystal clear when sharing it with others!

'Search me, O God, and know my heart' (Psalm 139:23).

------------------ **34** ------------------

Warnings and encouragements (1)

Luke 12:1-21

Luke now brings together various sayings of Jesus which
were possibly not spoken at the same time, nor even
necessarily in the order given here. The connecting link
is that when put together they form a series of warnings
and encouragements. Matthew 24:35 tells us why every
one of them is relevant to us today. We shall cover the
whole passage (ending at Luke 13:9) in the course of the
next three studies.

Be warned! — Truth will out
The besetting sin of the Pharisees was hypocrisy; glance

through Matthew 23:13-29 and make a careful note of
how many times Jesus denounced them for this. But
while hypocrisy (pretending to be what we are not) may
deceive others, it can never deceive God (as Hebrews
4:13 makes perfectly clear) and on the Day of Judgement
the whole truth will be fully and finally revealed. Notice
Paul's solemn words in Romans 2:16 and with those
words in mind turn to Peter's instructions in 1 Peter 1:17.

Be encouraged! — God counts sparrows
Having pointed out that God's judgement is so certain
and so infallible, Jesus went on to emphasize another
point. Even the fear of martyrdom should give way
before the fear of God, because even the most vicious
tyrants' power is limited. There comes a point at which
they 'can do no more' (v.4). On the other hand, God has
power not only to put an end to physical life but also to
condemn a man to eternal punishment in hell (v.5). We
should be more afraid of losing God's favour than of
losing our lives! Yet this 'fear' of God is not terror,
because God is a God of amazing love and infinite care,
as Jesus now illustrated by his reference to the sparrows
(vv.6,7). Sparrows normally sold at two for a penny
(Matthew 10:29), but there seemed to be a discount for
quantity, which meant that if you bought four, you got
an extra one free! (v.6) Yet God's providential care
extends even to creatures of such little value: 'Not one of
them is forgotten by God' (v.6). As for human beings,
God is intimately concerned about the minutest detail of
our lives (v.7). That being so, we should never be
ashamed of him (vv.8,9) and be assured that if we find
ourselves in a situation in which we are being persecuted
for righteousness' sake, we can rely on the guidance and
enabling of the Holy Spirit (vv.11,12).

Be warned! — There is an unforgivable sin
The Holy Spirit's great ministry is to bear witness to the

truth about Jesus Christ (see John 16:13,14). To blaspheme against the Holy Spirit is to reject his witness altogether. When a person continues to do that there is no hope for him, because he is rejecting God's only way of salvation. Verse 10 has caused many people great distress because they have misunderstood its meaning; but the person who is anxious that he may have committed the unforgivable sin has almost certainly not done so, or he would have no sorrow or concern about displeasing God or rejecting the clear witness that he gives about his Son.

Be warned! — Greed is insane

At this point a man seems to have interrupted Jesus, asking him to arbitrate in a family squabble over inheritance (v.13). Jesus firmly refused to get involved (v.14), but took the opportunity of pointing out that possessions do not make a man rich (make a careful note of v.15). He drove his point home with a simple but telling parable (vv.16-20). Greed is insane, because we will lose all our material possessions the moment we die, and that may be 'this very night'! (v.20) Proverbs 11:4 will then put all our riches in context.

'Set your minds on things above, not on earthly things' (Colossians 3:2).

35

Warnings and encouragements (2)

Luke 12:22-48

Today's reading takes in the second of three sections in
this part of Luke's Gospel, in which he records various
sayings of Jesus which, when taken together, form a
series of warnings and encouragements.

Be encouraged! — Your Father is a King
In warning people about greed, Jesus had told a parable
about a wealthy and successful farmer (vv.16-21). But
wealth can be a stumbling-block not only to the rich but
to the poor. One is tempted to gloat and the other to fret;
one sins because of the lot he has and the other over the
little he has. Yet Jesus taught that it was wrong to be
anxious, even about necessities. The whole lesson of
verses 22-34 could be summed up in one phrase: 'Do not
worry' (v.22). Verse 25 illustrates the futility of worry
very well. Nobody can extend his life by worrying about
it; as a matter of fact, the reverse is almost certainly what
would happen! Jesus backed up his arguments with a
number of simple illustrations from nature. The birds of
the air (v.24) and the flowers and grass in the fields
(vv.27,28) are vivid examples of God's amazing and
adequate provision. The Bible does not encourage
Christians to be lazy or careless or to rely on others for
their maintenance (notice carefully what Paul says in 2
Thessalonians 3:7-12) but we must marry our personal

responsibility to God's permanent reliability and remember that as far as the necessities of life are concerned, our Father knows what we need (v.30). What is more, he has promised to give us not only these earthly things, but the kingdom of God itself (v.32). It is therefore quite wrong for us to be 'afraid' (v.32). On the contrary, our only concern should be that we seek this kingdom by living godly, obedient lives. God promises that if we make that our concern he will make all the other things his concern — which is a cast-iron guarantee that we shall receive all that we need (v.31).

Be encouraged! — Jesus is coming

The Christian has yet another motive for sitting loose to material possessions — Jesus is coming back and may do so at any time (v.40). That being so, we should be constantly on the alert (vv.35,36). John sums up what this will mean in terms of our daily lives (1 John 3:2,3). When that great event occurs, the faithful and obedient servants will receive a reward that Jesus described in the most astonishing terms (v.37), though we are not given any detailed explanation of what this will mean. No wonder Jesus said that at that day, 'It will be good for those servants' (v.37).

Be warned! — Servants are accountable

After hearing this parable, Peter appeared to ask whether it referred to all Christians, or just to the inner circle of apostles (v.41). To answer his question, Jesus told another parable, the gist of which could be summed up like this: while all servants are responsible, those with special privileges have special responsibilities. In the parable, the 'faithful and wise manager' (v.42) was promoted as a reward for his services. But if a man in the same position of authority had misused his office (v.45) he would be severely punished (v.46). Knowledge, responsibility and accountability go together and we

must give serious weight to everything the Bible has to
say about God's perfect justice, both in granting rewards
and in administering punishment (vv.47,48). Notice how
this is put in James 3:1 and 4:17.

'Those who have been given a trust must prove faithful' (1
Corinthians 4:2)

36

Warnings and
encouragements (3)

Luke 12:49-13:9

Today's reading completes the section beginning at Luke
12:1, in which Jesus issues a number of warnings and at
the same time gives words of encouragement to his
followers. These final verses cover five main truths, all of
them in the nature of warnings.

Be warned! — Truth divides

Verses 49-53 are a sobering reminder that genuine
Christianity has radical consequences. When Jesus spoke
of his coming 'baptism' and added, 'And how distressed
I am until it is completed' (v.50), he was referring to his
crucifixion (compare Mark 10:33,34) which would over-
whelm him with grief (see Matthew 26:38; Luke 22:44).
While that great sacrifice would save multitudes of
people, it would also lead to 'fire' (v.49) and 'division'
(v.51). This is a difficult passage to analyse in a clear yet
concise way, but there does seem to be one obvious way
in which 'fire' and 'division' can be linked together. As

Christians began to make a moral and spiritual impact on society, men would become inflamed with opposition to the gospel and there would even be times when persecution for the gospel's sake would divide members of the same family from each other (vv.52,53). This kind of opposition may be hard to bear and difficult to understand, but we must remember that in his perfect wisdom God allows persecution in order that his church might be purified (see 1 Peter 1:6,7).

Be warned! — History is speaking

Some of the Jews seemed to be good amateur weather-forecasters! (Link v.54 with Matthew 16:2,3.) But Jesus told them that whatever their skill at interpreting the clouds and the wind, they were hopelessly ignorant of the things that really mattered (v.56). The Christian should live with his newspaper in one hand and his Bible in the other, and learn to interpret the first in the light of the second!

Be warned! — The Judge is waiting

Jesus next pointed out that some people were so taken up with trivialities that they had lost all sense of proportion and judgement (v.57). They had even become careless about their own standing in God's sight. Jesus compared them to a man and his accuser on their way to court (v.58). As the man concerned is clearly in the wrong — hence the likely sentence (vv.58,59) — the sensible attitude to adopt to the accuser is to 'be reconciled to him on the way' (v.58). In the same way, the certainty of condemnation should make a man look to God for mercy before he has to face his inevitable justice (link Psalm 2:12 with Acts 3:19).

Be warned! — Repentance is essential

This follows on perfectly. When someone told Jesus of the massacre of certain Jews on Pilate's instructions

(13:1) he added another headline incident — the collapse
of a building in Jerusalem (v.4) — and then issued a
stern warning. Those who had died were no worse than
other people (vv.2,4); but their sudden deaths should be
a reminder to everyone of the necessity and urgency of
repentance (vv.3,5).

Be warned! — There comes a last chance

This 'warning' section comes to an end with a tiny but
telling parable (vv.6-9). The fig tree should have
produced fruit, because it was planted in the fertile
soil of a vineyard (v.6). Yet in three years it produced
nothing and instructions were given to cut it down
(v.7). The man who took care of the vineyard was
able to secure just one year's stay of execution (v.8)
but after that, judgement would be carried out (v.9).
The Jews should have recognized the primary reference as being to their own nation (see Jeremiah 24:1-3,
Hosea 9:10) but the issue is not only national but
personal. For some men, at a given moment of time,
there may be another chance; for all men, there comes a
last chance.

'Be merciful to me. O Lord' (Psalm 31:9).

37

Keys of the kingdom (1)

Luke 13:10-21

When John the Baptist was preparing the way for the coming of Jesus, he told his hearers, 'The kingdom of heaven is near' (Matthew 3:2), while Jesus himself could not have been clearer about the significance of his ministry when he announced that 'The kingdom of God has come upon you' (Matthew 12:28). Many of the things Jesus said and did can be most easily understood when we read them in the context of the kingdom of God and we will do this for our two remaining studies in Luke 13.

The overall spirit of the kingdom

While living in his home town of Nazareth, Jesus had been a regular worshipper at the local synagogue (see Luke 4:16) and he often taught in synagogues in the course of his itinerant ministry (see Mark 1:39). At this point in his life the opposition to him was mounting, with the result that this is the last recorded visit he paid to a synagogue. One sabbath day he saw a crippled woman in the congregation. Full of compassion for her, he called her over and immediately cured her of a disease that had gripped her for eighteen years (v.13). The ruler of the synagogue (the official responsible for all that went on there) complained to the people, suggesting that if there were others who needed healing, they should come on some other day of the week! (v.14) The reason for his outburst was that Jewish leaders had added to God's law about the sabbath a mass of complicated regulations and under these man-made laws Jesus could be accused of working and therefore breaking the Fourth Commandment (see Exodus 20:9-11). In reply, Jesus accused the ruler of blatant hypocrisy (v.15). Their sabbath laws allowed the Jews to have mercy on thirsty animals; surely it was within the spirit of God's law for Jesus to have mercy on this suffering woman? (vv.15-16) The kingdom of God is concerned with more important things than man-made religious paraphernalia (see Romans 14:17; Colossians 2:20) and with nothing more important than the overthrow of the devil (link v.16 with Hebrews 2:14,15).

The ultimate success of the kingdom
Jesus then told two tiny 'kingdom of God' parables, both taken from ordinary, everyday life. A 'mustard seed' (v.19) is very small (see what is said about it in Mark 4:31), but in favourable Middle East conditions it grows rapidly into a plant big enough to be called a tree (v.19). Jesus was making the point that, whatever opposition it faced, the kingdom of God was invincible and people from all nations would eventually become part of it (look ahead to v.29). Old Testament scholars would perhaps have remembered prophecies like Ezekiel 17:22-24, which used birds as a symbol for the nations of the world, and to those words we can add the marvellous promise of Isaiah 53:10,11. Whatever men might try to do to stop it, God has guaranteed the triumph of his gospel kingdom!

The inner strength of the kingdom
In the second parable, Jesus said that the kingdom of God was like 'yeast' (v.21). The woman concerned had a large amount of flour, but the apparently insignificant yeast would quietly penetrate it all (v.21). The picture is

clear: Christians are meant to penetrate society for Christ, changing its moral texture by the powerful influence of God-energized lives. In the worlds of politics, education, sport, music, medicine, art and other areas of social life, we should be quietly and humbly at work. The Christian minority made a great impact in the early days of the church (see Acts 17:6) and Christians have often pioneered enormous social changes down the years. We dare not opt out of our responsibilities in this whole area.

'God. . . calls you into his kingdom and glory' (1 Thessalonians 2:12).

38

Keys of the kingdom (2)

Luke 13:22-35

As Luke continues to record a number of scattered incidents, he reminds us that they all took place as Jesus was gradually making his way towards Jerusalem (v.22). Today's reading takes in three incidents that probably occurred at quite different times.

The priority Jesus urged
The teaching in this section (vv.22-30) was given in answer to a very important question (v.23). The Jews were constantly discussing this very point, although many of them believed that the kingdom of God was theirs by right of inheritance (see John 8:31-33, for

instance). In his reply Jesus ignored the statistical point
(*how many* would be saved) and concentrated on the
spiritual (*who* would be saved). Many who imagine that
they will be saved because of some vague association
with Jesus (v.26) will in fact be lost (v.27). Elsewhere we
are told of others with even higher hopes but who will
also be excluded from heaven (see Matthew 7:21-23). No
wonder Paul says what he does in 2 Corinthians 13:5!
Jesus made it clear that the door of the kingdom of God
was 'narrow' and a man must 'make every effort' to enter
(v.24). This does not mean that a man is saved by self-
effort — Jesus said exactly the opposite at the end of
verse 24 — but that salvation is a matter of extreme
urgency. The day will come when the door will be closed
and·it will be too late (v.25). It will then be especially
galling for proud but unconverted Jews to see Gentiles
from all over the world inside the kingdom of God (v.29)
and they themselves shut out. The challenge of these
verses can be put in the form of two questions: Are you
in? Are you trying to bring others in?

The purpose Jesus maintained

Luke next records some of the Pharisees warning Jesus of
an assassination attempt by Herod (v.31). Herod had
already been disturbed by reports of Jesus' ministry. At
one stage he even thought that Jesus must be a
reincarnation of John the Baptist, whom he had put to
death (the story is told in Mark 6:14-29; link this with
Luke 9:7-9). The Pharisees' warning may therefore have
been a false but deliberate 'leak' to frighten Jesus out of
Herod's territory of Galilee. Be that as it may, Jesus
replied that nothing could prevent his life from running
its God-appointed course, which would come to a climax
with his death at Jerusalem (v.33). A recurring spirit of
'I must' ran through the life of Jesus (see, for instance,
Luke 2:49; John 9:4) and it was this sense of divine
purpose that garrisoned his spirit against all opposition.

Every Christian can go through life with the same certainty, based on truths like those expressed in Psalm 139 and especially verses 5-10.

The plea Jesus made

Matthew places the words of verses 34 and 35 some time later, when Jesus was already at Jerusalem (Matthew 23:37-39). Luke probably inserted them here because of the mention of Jerusalem in verse 33. The city had a shocking record of violence against God's special messengers (see 2 Chronicles 24:21; 36:15-17, for instance). Yet those messengers had been tokens of God's mercy and even now Jesus would gladly have welcomed the people of the city into his protective care (v.34). But by and large they were 'not willing' (v.34). The outcome was to be appalling. The words of verse 35 were fulfilled literally when Jerusalem was destroyed in A.D.70 and in the same way the man who rejects Christ is left with nothing (see John 6:53). Like the rest of the world, Jerusalem would have to recognize Jesus at his second coming (v.35), but by then it would be too late (compare Matthew 24:30). It is always costly to reject God's mercy.

'Today, if you hear his voice, do not harden your hearts' (Hebrews 3:7,8).

39

Words of wisdom

Luke 14:1-24

Even his enemies were often struck by the sheer moral
power of Christ's teaching (compare Luke 4:22 with
Matthew 13:54). What made his words even more
striking was the fact that they were not all carefully
prepared speeches or sermons. The setting for today's
reading, for instance, is a meal in the house of a
prominent Pharisee (v.1). But in the course of it Jesus
had words for everyone who was present — and for all of
us, who were not!

A word for the critics

As we saw earlier, Jesus constantly infuriated the
Pharisees by healing people on the sabbath day (glance
back to 6:6-11 and 13:10-17). Faced with yet another
man in dire need — the word 'dropsy' (v.2) means that
the man's body was hideously swollen with excess fluid
— Jesus asked the watching Pharisees a question
(v.3). Getting no answer, he healed the man (v.4) and
immediately asked another unanswerable question
(vv.5,6). We may not always be able to please ecclesiastical fuss-pots, but we can rest assured that Spirit-filled
living is never in conflict with God's law! (See Galatians
5:22;23.)

A word for the guests

As the meal was about to be served, Jesus noticed some of the guests worming their way into the most important places (v.7). This prompted him to tell a simple but pointed parable (vv.8-10). The maxim in verse 11 appears again in Matthew 23:12 and Luke 18:14 and the same truth is stated many times in the Old Testament (Proverbs 29:23, for instance). Pride makes a man small, however great he may seem to be; humility makes a man great, however small he may seem to be. The lesson is easy to learn, but difficult to live. James 4:10 should help!

A word for the host

The meal seems to have been something of a closed shop, part of an endless round of invitations involving the same people. Jesus had a comment on this too (vv.12-14). The words in verse 12 do not mean that a man should refuse hospitality to his family or friends, but rather that his kindness should also benefit those with no means of repaying him. That kind of giving is a real test of a man's generosity and it will be rewarded with God's blessing (v.14). The Bible makes specific promises to those who are generous to the poor (see Proverbs 19:17, for instance).

A word for the lost

Many Jews believed that the Messiah's coming would be marked by a gigantic feast and the words Jesus used moved one man to burst out with joyful anticipation of the event (v.15), no doubt confident that as a Jew his own place was reserved! In reply, Jesus told what we might call 'the parable of the excuses'. Invitations to banquets were issued in two stages (compare vv.16,17 with Esther 5:8; 6:14). In the parable, the invited guests began to cry off when the second invitation came. But they gave excuses rather than reasons. Would a man buy a field before he had seen it? (v.18) Could the oxen not be

tested a day or so later? (v.19) Could the newly-wed not
bring his wife? (v.20) Grieved at their refusal, the host
sent his servant first into the city and then into the
countryside, freely inviting the most unlikely people until
his house was filled with guests (vv.21-23). The lesson
was this: throughout the Old Testament God's prophets
had been calling the people of Israel. Now Jesus was
bringing the second, urgent invitation (notice Hebrews
1:1,2). Yet the privileged Jews were rejecting it (compare
John 5:39,40). As a result, many Gentiles (not directly
included in the first invitation) would gladly accept the
call to the feast and enter the kingdom of God (see
Romans 9:22-26).

'Go into all the world and preach the good news. . . ' (Mark
16:15).

------------------------------ **40** ------------------------------

Discipleship

Luke 14:25-35

Although the incidents in this part of Luke's narrative
are sometimes unconnected and out of exact chrono-
logical order, they are all in the general context of Jesus
making his way to Jerusalem (glance back to 9:51). This
may explain the large crowds who now flocked after him
(v.25). Many must have thought that he was about to
take the city by storm, throw out the Roman occupying
forces and set up an earthly kingdom. But nothing could
have been further from the truth! (See John 18:36.) Jesus

was on his way to be crucified, not crowned, and Christianity was to be no easy ride in the wake of a revolutionary folk hero. To drive this lesson home, Jesus suddenly stopped his enthusiastic followers in their tracks (notice the word 'turning' in v.25) and solemnly laid down the terms of Christian discipleship. He said that there were conditions to be met, without which a man could not be his disciple (vv.26,27,33). His threefold use of the phrase 'cannot be my disciple' points us to the specific conditions he mentioned.

The prior claim

The words of verse 26 do not mean that we must literally hate the members of our own family. Apart from being an absurd religious requirement, this would flatly contradict one of the Ten Commandments (see Exodus 20:12) and Jesus said that he had come not to destroy the law but to fulfil it (Matthew 5:17). In the sense in which it is used here, the word 'hate' means to love less. There is a good example of this in the Old Testament (see Genesis 29:31-33). To be a true disciple of Jesus means that whenever there is a conflict of claims, his takes priority. This may produce difficulties (notice the three verses that come before Matthew's version of this teaching in Matthew 10:34-36) but there is no obedient alternative. Acts 5:29 puts the issue precisely!

The painful cross

Verse 27 is simple but searching; compare it with 9:23 and remember that we noticed the word 'daily' there. Jesus was not, of course, suggesting that only Christians put to death on a cross would rank as genuine disciples, yet the picture he used was a vivid one. A man carrying his cross to the place of execution had no further plans of his own; he would have forfeited control of his life. In the same way, the true disciple is marked by spiritual self-crucifixion, which can sometimes be agonizingly painful.

To die to our own comforts, ambitions and plans is of the very essence of true Christianity. Paul puts it perfectly in Galatians 2:20.

The premeditated cost

Jesus next told two brief parables (vv.28-32). He applied their message by saying that a disciple must 'give up everything he has' (v.33). The precise linking of this phrase to the parables is not immediately obvious, but the gist of the teaching is clear: no man can afford to think lightly about being a Christian. A disciple must be prepared to pay any price in order to please his Lord and Saviour and at the same time abandon all trust in his own resources and ability. (Read Mark 8:34-38 for another expression of the same line of teaching.) Luke now inserts Jesus' parable about salt (compare vv.34,35 with Matthew 5:13 and Mark 9:50). Salt was used as a preservative, as flavouring and as a fertilizer. The inferior salt used in those days sometimes lost its saltiness by exposure to the elements and when it did so it was virtually useless. In the same way, the Christian disciple whose character becomes diluted with world-liness completely loses his effectiveness. Christians should penetrate the world without ever becoming part of it. It was to help them to do so that Jesus prayed as he did at John 17:15.

'A student is not above his teacher' (Matthew 10:24).

41

Lost and found (1)

Luke 15:1-10

This chapter of Luke's Gospel is taken up by three
parables with the same theme. In today's study we shall
look at the first two of these well-known stories. In trying
to understand the meaning of these parables it is
important to notice the circumstances in which Jesus
originally told them. The situation was that 'tax-
collectors and "sinners" were all gathering around to
hear him' (v.1). Tax-collectors were despised by the Jews
not only because they were employed by the Romans,
but because many of them swindled their own people by
over-charging (Luke 19:8 hints at this sort of thing). The
'sinners' were people who had no interest in the finer
points of religious law, which the Pharisees considered
all-important. To them, these people were just an
ignorant and godless rabble (see John 7:45-49). That is
why we read of their reaction in verse 2. How could Jesus
possibly be a man of God if he associated so freely with
the country's riff-raff? Little did they realize it, but their
miserable muttering was to trigger off some of the most
wonderful teaching in the New Testament!

The lost sheep
The first parable (vv.3-6) asked a question to which
there could only be one answer. It would be obvious to
everybody that the shepherd's active concern would be

for the one sheep astray in dangerous 'open country'
(v.4) and he would do everything he could to recover it.
When he found it, he would gladly carry it home (v.5).
In that part of the world, flocks tended to be quite small,
so that even one sheep would be very valuable. This
meant that when the lost animal was safely back in the
flock it was cause for great celebration (v.6). Jesus then
drew out the lesson of the parable (v.7). There are
several quite reasonable interpretations of the phrase
'ninety-nine righteous persons who do not need to
repent' (v.7). It may well be that Jesus was making a
thinly-veiled reference to the self-righteous Pharisees (see
18:11 for an example of this). Be that as it may, the
central thing Jesus wanted to get across was that God
was lovingly concerned for lost sinners and rejoiced when
they turned from their sin.

The lost silver
The second parable (vv.8,9) was equally simple. The
'ten silver coins' (v.8) may have formed a married
woman's head-dress or necklace (the equivalent of
today's wedding ring) or they may have been used as
currency, one such coin being the equivalent of a day's
wage for a working man. The original word, *drachma*, is
still in use in Greece today. In either case, sentimentally
or commercially, the piece of silver was valuable and
important to the owner and when she discovered that it
was missing she began a thorough search of the house
(v.8). Having told the story, Jesus added the same
postscript as he did to the first one: one sinner turning
from his sin was a cause for great rejoicing in heaven
(v.10). Taken together, then, these two parables teach
two great truths, both of which would have staggered the
supercilious Pharisees. The first was that God is lovingly
concerned to reach out to those who have rejected him
and gone their own, sinful way (compare Ezekiel 33:11;
Luke 19:10); the second is that God welcomes with open

arms the worst sinners who honestly turn to him for
forgiveness (see 2 Peter 3:9). To the Christian there are
two incidental but important lessons. The first is that he
should show genuine love for even the unloveliest of
people. Romans 13:8 has something pretty startling
to say about that! The second is that he should
unjudgingly welcome all Christians, even those with
obvious deficiencies, as brothers and sisters in Christ,
and Romans 14:1 has a helpful comment on that.

'God our Saviour. . . wants all men to be saved and to come to a
knowledge of the truth' (1 Timothy 2:3,4).

----------- **42** -----------

Lost and found (2)

Luke 15:11-32

We come now to one of the most familiar stories in the
whole Bible, usually called the parable of the prodigal
son. There are many ways in which it can be approached
and analysed; in this study we shall use five words to
hold together the main thread of the story.

Rebellion
According to Jewish law, the younger of two sons would
be entitled to one-third of his father's estate (see
Deuteronomy 21:17). The division of the property and
goods was usually made after the father's death, but in
this case the self-willed son demanded his rights in
advance (v.12). Soon afterwards, he left for some far-off

country, where he 'squandered his wealth in wild living'
(v.13).

Ruin
We are not told how long this wild extravagance went on,
but eventually he ran out of money (v.14). Even worse,
the country in which he was living was hit by a terrible
famine (v.14). With an empty purse and empty stomach,
he looked for work, but the only job available was
looking after pigs (v.15). Nothing could have been more
disgusting for a Jew, to whom the pig was 'unclean' by
law (see Leviticus 11:7; Deuteronomy 14:8). Things got
so bad that he would gladly have eaten 'the pods [of the
carob tree] that the pigs were eating' (v.16). There is a
high cost in low living. Psalm 34:21 is just one of the
many places where the Bible makes this solemnly clear.

Reflection
When he was at rock bottom, the young man finally
'came to his senses' (v.17). Even his father's servants
were better off than he was (v.17). He would go back
home, confess his stupidity and sin, and ask to be
employed as a servant (vv.18,19).

Repentance
Notice carefully that he immediately put his thoughts
and words into action: 'He got up and went to his father'
(v.20). Repentance means more than recognizing sin, or
even regretting it; it means forsaking sin and turning to
God. Look up Matthew 3:7,8 and notice how John the
Baptist dealt with those who wanted acceptance without
repentance! Even as Christians we need to remember
that until a person forsakes a sin, God will not forgive it.

Reception
Verses 20-24 are the real heart of the story, showing the
father's loving forgiveness as immediate (v.20), com-

passionate (v.20) and extravagantly generous (vv.22-24).
Many fanciful interpretations have been given to other
details of the story, but we must remember that a parable
was normally told to illustrate one main point. A parable
is a window, not an exhibition of coloured glass! As with
the stories of the lost sheep and the lost silver, Jesus
wanted to illustrate the overwhelming love of God. The
Old Testament had already taught this (see Deuteronomy 30:1-3 for instance); now God was to demonstrate
it in the most amazing way. But the parable was not yet
finished. The elder son was furious at the reception his
brother received (vv.25-28) and told his father the reason
in no uncertain terms (vv.29,30). His father's only
response was to assure him that he, too, had his undying
and open-handed love. The challenge to the Pharisees
was obvious, as it should be obvious to us. There is no
place for peevishness, envy, jealousy or pride in God's
family. Let us rejoice at his goodness to others and at his
goodness to us, remembering that in neither case is it
ever the result of merit on our part, but always of mercy
on his! To reject those whom God has accepted or to
imagine that we deserve from God better treatment than
others are equally wrong attitudes.

'The Lord, the Lord, the compassionate and gracious God'
(Exodus 34:6).

---------------------- **43** ----------------------

Money matters (1)

Luke 16:1-13

The previous chapter of Luke's Gospel contained three
well-known parables; this one contains two that are less
familiar. The subject in chapter 15 was God's love for
sinners; here it is basically man's use of wealth. The first
of these two parables is very difficult to understand with
precision, but the following summary would fit the facts
as we have them. A rich man received a report that his
manager was swindling him (v.1), possibly by adding a
certain amount to loans on which interest was already
being charged, and then pocketing the difference when
the loans were repaid. Threatened with dismissal and
unemployment (v.3), the manager hit on a crafty scheme
to get the debtors on his side (v.4). Quickly summoning
them one at a time, he authorized them to reduce the
amounts they owed — amounts that were apparently
payable in kind rather than in cash. For example, a man
who owed 'eight hundred gallons of olive oil' (v.6) was
told to reduce it by half. Another man, whose debt was
valued at 'a thousand bushels of wheat' (v.7), was told to
call it eight hundred. It was a brilliant move, because the
debtors were now in his debt! What is more, if we have
the outline of the story right, his master was also in some
difficulty, as he was breaking the Old Testament law
about lending money (see Exodus 22:25, for example).
Unable to press the matter any further, he 'commended

the dishonest manager because he had acted shrewdly'
(v.8). From this whole murky business Jesus drew out
four lessons about man's use of wealth.

A lesson about shrewdness

Jesus commented on the remarkable shrewdness of
ordinary, unconverted people 'in dealing with their
own kind' (v.8). While we must never imitate their
dishonesty, it is a great loss to the kingdom of God when
Christians are slipshod and careless about their use of
time, gifts and possessions. Compare 'the people of light'
in verse 8 with John 12:36 and Ephesians 5:8.

A lesson about sharing

Jesus went on to say that we should use our 'worldly
wealth' in such a way that at the end of life we will be
'welcomed into eternal dwellings' (v.9). Money given to
evangelism and other Christian work will then be seen to
have been an investment paying enormous and eternal
dividends (notice what Jesus said in Matthew 6:20;
19:21).

A lesson about stewardship

This was brought home by one statement and two
questions. The statement is very telling (v.10). A man's
character is shown in everything he does, not just by the
big things. Even little actions speak louder than words.
The questions make a direct challenge. Basically, the
first question (v.11) asks this: if we are deficient in the
way we use an ordinary thing like money, how can we
expect God to entrust us with 'true riches'? The second
question presses home the same principle from an
entirely different angle. Everything we handle here on
earth is really 'someone else's property' (v.12), see 1
Chronicles 29:14 and 1 Corinthians 6:19,20 for the
owner's identity! If we handle these things badly, how
can we expect to receive those everlasting riches

promised to faithful stewards? (Compare Matthew
25:23.) Our temporary stewardship will determine our
permanent ownership.

A lesson about servitude
This is in verse 13. A servant was in fact a slave,
completely owned by his master, to whom he owed total
allegiance. But the principle extends beyond that particular relationship. Deep in his heart, a man can only be
committed in one direction — towards God or away from
him, and the man preoccupied with money cannot
possibly be a man of God.

'Do not store up for yourselves treasures on earth' (Matthew
6:19).

44

Money matters (2)

Luke 16:14-31

This passage follows directly on from the end of our last
study, in which Jesus told the story about the shrewd
manager and then drew some challenging conclusions
about man's use of wealth. The Pharisees to whom
Jesus was speaking 'loved money' (v.14) and it is
therefore no surprise to read that when he began to
probe in that area they 'were sneering at him' (v.14).
But that kind of behaviour is often just a smoke-screen
to cover up the truth and Jesus quickly exposed them
as hypocrites. In particular, he pointed out that what

☐ I have understood the Good News, and said the prayer, and want to become a Christian.

☐ I am interested in Jesus Christ and would like to know more about becoming a Christian.

NAME _____

ADDRESS _____

_____

_____

Windsor + Eton

riverside

direct line

end of line.

expect 2 trains a
hour. 15 mi journey.

5 mi walk.
ask direction.
cross river
High St → old church.

is 'highly valued among men' — that is, the accumulation of wealth regardless of how it is gained or how it is used — is 'detestable in God's sight' (v.15). Link this with Jeremiah 22:13-15. Jesus then underlined his statement in two ways.

A principle about life

The Pharisees may have been furious at a 'layman' like Jesus daring to teach God's law to them, the self-professed experts (see John 7:15, for instance, and the answer Jesus gave them in the following verse!) but Jesus calmly pointed out that while John the Baptist's preaching marked the end of the Old Testament era (v.16), God's moral law remained unchanged (v.17). Throughout his ministry Jesus made it clear that he had not come to destroy the law, but to fulfil it (see Matthew 5:17). Jesus completed God's law; the Pharisees corrupted it. The matter of divorce was an example of this. The law allowed a man to divorce his wife under certain circumstances (Deuteronomy 24:1-4). But some people stretched these conditions to include things as trivial as the woman speaking to a strange man or ruining her husband's meal! Jesus swept all these ridiculous interpretations aside and underlined God's original intention for his people, namely the sanctity, security and permanence of the marriage bond (read v.18 together with Matthew 19:3-9 where Jesus shows that the principle goes back *before* the law of Moses). The principles of honesty and charity are equally part of God's permanent law for a man's life.

A parable about death

The parable concerns two men. One was wealthy and self-indulgent: he 'lived in luxury every day' (v.19). The other man was a beggar called Lazarus, tormented by hunger, disease and scavenging dogs (vv.20,21). But, for all his poverty, the beggar obviously possessed the riches of living faith (see James 2:5) because when he died he went to heaven (v.22). The rich man, on the other hand, lived and died without God and went to hell (vv.22,23). The extraordinary conversation he had with Abraham reveals certain facts about the condition of a person who is in hell: he is 'in torment' (v.23); he can in some way 'see' heaven (v.23); he longs for relief from his agony (v.24); he can remember his life on earth (v.25); he recognizes the need for people on earth to hear the gospel (vv.27,28) and he knows that repentance is essential (v.30). But it is all too late: between heaven and hell 'a great chasm has been fixed' (v.26) and there is no traffic between the two. Notice what Jesus said in Matthew 25:46. After death, *all* men are eternally secure — the righteous in heaven and the unrighteous in hell! And what was the rich man's damning sin? He indulged his own selfish appetite day after day and ignored a starving beggar on his doorstep. No story could illustrate more clearly that the Bible's teaching on man's use of wealth is meant to be taken seriously. Statements like those in Proverbs 21:13, James 4:17 and 1 John 3:17 are not just indications of our responsibility to help those in need; they are literally matters of life and death!

'He who gives to the poor will lack nothing' (Proverbs 28:27).

45

Teaching, preaching
and healing

Luke 17:1-19

At the beginning of his public ministry, we are told that Jesus 'went throughout Galilee teaching. . . preaching the good news of the kingdom, and healing every disease and sickness among the people' (Matthew 4:23). Now, after nearly three years, and with the shadow of his death growing larger every day, we find him still engaged up to the hilt in his God-ordained ministry. No wonder he was able to say what he did in John 17:4!

Teaching

There are three pieces of teaching in the early part of this chapter. The first is about causing people to sin (vv.1,2; compare Mark 9:42). In a fallen world, temptation is inevitable (v.1), but those who put temptation in other people's way face certain and terrible judgement (v.2). By 'these little ones' Jesus probably meant all Christians, old as well as young — a beautiful example of his loving care for them. Compare Matthew 18:14 and Luke 12:32 and notice how in 1 John 5:21 John followed his Master's example. Next came teaching about forgiveness (vv.3,4). Sin is not to be treated lightly. If a man sins we must 'rebuke him', but if he repents we must forgive him' (v.3). 'Seven times in a day' (v.4) does not mean that we count the number of times we forgive; it means we forgive until we lose count! Compare Matthew 18:21,22;

our forgiveness is to be governed by compassion, not by computer! The third piece of teaching is about our duty to God (vv.7-10). In a nutshell, the lesson is that we can never claim to put God in our debt (v.10). Link up Psalm 96:8, Ecclesiastes 12:13, Matthew 5:48 and Mark 12:30. When we have exceeded these we will have exceeded our duty! In the light of that fact, who can dare to lift his head in pride?

Preaching
This came in response to a request from the disciples (v.5). The good news Jesus declared was amazing (v.6). Faith links our impotence to God's omnipotence and when that is in operation, anything can happen — and to 'mountains' as well as 'trees' (see Matthew 17:20). Faith and victory are inseparable in the Christian life (see 1 John 5:14).

Healing
The story of the miraculous healing of ten lepers (vv.11-19) is exclusive to Luke. The lepers were standing 'at a distance' because of long-established quarantine laws (see Leviticus 13:45,46); notice that they had to shout in order to be heard (v.13). The story is told without comment, but there is an important lesson in it. Notice that in verse 14 Jesus told the lepers to go and show themselves to the priests, who were authorized to pronounce a cured leper 'clean' (see Leviticus 14:1-32, and especially verse 7). His instructions must have seemed crazy, if not cruel — after all, the men were still covered with leprosy — but the lepers did as they were told and 'as they went, they were cleansed' (v.14). Mark that carefully! Only when they exercised faith did the miracle happen. But now a sour note creeps into the story. Of the ten men healed, only one, a Samaritan returned to give thanks to Jesus (v.16) and to praise God for his goodness (v.15). Jesus pointed this out by means

of two questions (vv.17,18), but the incident only illustrates the truth that ingratitude towards God is the mark of most of humanity (see Romans 1:21). The grateful Samaritan received a further word from Jesus (v.19) and it may be that he received the added and greater blessing of salvation (compare Mark 10:52). Are you as thankful as you should be, or do you tend to take God's goodness for granted? Are you constantly obeying 1 Thessalonians 5:18?

'It is a good thing to praise the Lord' (Psalm 92:1).

46

The coming of the kingdom of God

Luke 17:20-37

The air was now full of rumour, discussion and speculation about 'the kingdom of God' (v.20) and this was hardly surprising. The Old Testament had been full of statements and prophecies about it, not least in connection with the coming Messiah (see Isaiah 9:6,7); John the Baptist had declared, 'The kingdom of heaven is near' (Matthew 3:2) and Jesus himself had told one parable after another to illustrate its nature. Against this background, the Pharisees' question in verse 20 may have been perfectly natural and innocent. In any event, it resulted in a straightforward statement to them and more detailed teaching to the disciples.

The King and the kingdom
The reply Jesus gave the Pharisees (v.21) probably meant something like 'The kingdom of God is in the midst of you,' meaning that Jesus himself was the personification of the kingdom of God. Not only were the words he spoke and the life he lived utterly different from those of any other man (see John 7:46); his whole personality was a living revelation of God (link John 1:14 and Colossians 2:9). The Pharisees were so spiritually blind that they were searching for the kingdom while looking at the King!

False kingdoms
Jesus now turned to his disciples and began by warning them of trouble to come. For himself, there would be suffering and rejection (v.25) when the powers of darkness would reign (look ahead to 22:53). For the disciples, things would get so difficult that they would 'long to see one of the days of the Son of Man' (v.22; compare Matthew 9:14,15). At the same time there would be all kinds of false dawns, promising the kingdom of God without producing it (compare vv.21 and 23 with Mark 13:21,22). This prophecy had been repeatedly fulfilled over the years and in many different ways. The kingdom of God is neither ecclesiastical, political nor social.

The real kingdom
The best way to deal with all these counterfeits is to realize that when 'the day of the Son of Man' (Christ's return to the earth) occurs, there will be no dispute about it. It will be as dazzling and definite as a flash of lightning (v.24) and will have immediate and unmistakable results (vv.34-36). The righteous will be taken up to be with the Lord (see 1 Thessalonians 4:17), while the unrighteous will be left to despair, judgement and doom.

The unexpected kingdom

The solemn challenge just given is made urgent by the fact that by its very suddenness, Christ's return will catch people unawares (vv.26-30). There is obviously nothing inherently sinful about the activities mentioned here, such as eating, drinking, marrying, buying, selling, planting and building, but the inference is that people will be wholly taken up with things like these. A man caught up with this world is not ready for the next one. Materialism is no preparation for judgement or for heaven. Colossians 3:1-4 points to a better way.

When the kingdom comes

With the warning, 'Remember Lot's wife' (v.32), Jesus reminded his disciples of one person who was reluctant to leave her earthly possessions (the story is told in Genesis 19:1-28, see especially vv.17,23-28). The true disciple will not think first of his possessions (v.31), nor even of his own life (v.33). All of this ties in exactly with what we saw earlier in 14:25-33). Verse 37 is notoriously difficult and over the years nearly sixty explanations of it have been given. Jesus may have meant that when the earth is ready for final judgement, that judgement will inevitably come. The same terrible truth is stated at Revelation 14:15.

'You too, be patient and stand firm, because the Lord's coming is near' (James 5:8).

47

Man's approach to God

Luke 18:1-17

At this point, Luke's narrative continues to read like a
colourful magazine, in which apparently unconnected
features are placed alongside each other by the editor.
This is certainly true about the early part of this chapter,
though there is some kind of connecting link if we see
each of the three sections as teaching one important truth
about man's approach to God, either in his primary need
of salvation or of a subsequent need of help in answer to
prayer. One word will crystallize each of the attitudes we
need to have.

Persistence
The purpose of the first parable in this chapter is stated
simply and clearly (v.1). As he seemed to constitute a
one-man court, the judge in the story was probably a
Roman (Jewish courts had three judges). He was
certainly godless and unscrupulous (v.2), as were many
Roman judges at that time. A certain widow in the town
'kept coming to him' (v.3), asking for justice in what
seems to have been a long-standing dispute. The judge
ignored her for a while (v.4), but finally gave in 'so that
she won't eventually wear me out with her coming!' (v.5)
The lesson Jesus drew from the parable was by way of
contrast. If even a corrupt judge is capable of granting
justice, surely God will 'bring about justice for his chosen

ones' (v.7). This has the same kind of ring about it as the statement made in 11:13. Christians will always be in the minority (notice the rhetorical question in verse 8) but our heavenly Father is gracious and generous and longs to give his children those things that will be for their blessing. This should give great encouragement to Christians to 'cry out to him day and night' (v.7).

Penitence

The purpose of the second parable is equally clear, as we are told in verse 9. It was spoken to condemn those who trusted in their own goodness. In the story, two men — a Pharisee and a tax-collector — went up to the temple to pray. But the Pharisee never got around to praying. He spent all his time boasting to God of his honesty, purity and generosity and his general moral superiority (vv.11,12). There is no reason to doubt that he was telling the truth, but his whole attitude was one of insufferable arrogance; in his own eyes he was head and shoulders above other men (v.11). The tax-collector, on the other hand, was totally different, in words and actions. He stood 'at a distance', bowed his head and beat upon his breast (a sign of grief, see 23:48). His only words were 'God, have mercy on me, a sinner' (v.13). Literally, he used the phrase '*the* sinner', as if he felt he was the worst sinner in the world (compare Paul's estimation of himself at 1 Timothy 1:15). But it was this man who went home 'justified', that is, right with God, for the reason given at the end of verse 14 (compare 14:11; Matthew 23:12). The man who is not penitent cannot be pardoned (see Matthew 9:13).

Dependence

The lovely little incident in verses 15-17 is also recorded by Matthew (19:13-15) and Mark (10:13-16), with minor differences in the wording. When some parents brought their babies to Jesus for his blessing (v.15), the disciples protested, no doubt trying to protect Jesus from what they thought were unimportant matters. It is interesting to notice that whenever they did that kind of thing Jesus overruled them (see 18:39,40; Matthew 15:23,24). Gladly welcoming the children, Jesus taught that a person could only receive the kingdom of God when he did so 'like a little child' (v.17), that is to say, in a spirit of unquestioning dependence on the goodness and mercy of God (notice how Jesus emphasized this in Matthew 18:1-3).

'It is good for me to be near God' (Psalm 73:28).

---------------------------------- **48** ----------------------------------

The Master at work

Luke 18:18-43

At the end of his Gospel, the apostle John says that if everything Jesus did while he was here on earth were written down, 'I suppose that even the whole world would not have room for the books that would be written' (John 21:25). That may be hyperbole, but it is impressive to notice how a small section of Luke's narrative such as today's reading contains a remarkable variety of work. We can get a general grasp of it by highlighting three particular things Jesus did.

The failure he revealed
The 'ruler' (v.18) — some kind of local official — asked a vitally important question (compare v.18 with 10:25) but

the most remarkable thing was the way he addressed
Jesus. '*Good* teacher' (v.18) was an unheard-of phrase, as
the Jews taught that only God and the law of God were
wholly good. This helps to explain the opening words of
Jesus' answer (v.19); the man was being challenged to
consider the implication of what he said. As the ruler
obviously thought he could be saved by his own
goodness, Jesus pointed him to some of the commandments (v.20). Amazing as it may seem, the ruler believed
that he had passed those tests (v.21). Without pausing
to correct him, Jesus instantly revealed the man's basic
flaw (vv.22,23): he put his goods before his God. When
Jesus commented on the problems posed by wealth
(compare vv.24,25 with 1 Timothy 6:9) the disciples
were astonished (v.26), not least because of a popular
belief that wealth was a sign of God's favour. In reply,
Jesus made a crucially important statement (link v.27
with Galatians 2:16). No man, rich or poor, can ever
achieve his own salvation; that power belongs exclusively
to God. When Peter remarked that he and the other
disciples had forsaken all to follow him (compare v.28
with 5:11), Jesus assured him that the Christian's
rewards would always exceed his sacrifices, both in this
life and in the life to come (vv.29,30 and see Mark 8:35).

The forecast he repeated
It is sometimes forgotten that as well as being a King
(John 18:37) and a Priest (Hebrews 4:14), Jesus was also
a Prophet (link Deuteronomy 18:18 with Matthew 21:11)
and, as a Prophet, he had authority both to forthtell and
foretell God's Word. In verses 31-33 he made another
forecast of his coming death and resurrection (compare
9:22). For the first time he spoke of being handed over to
'the Gentiles' (v.32) — a clear reference to the fact that
the Romans would carry out his torture and execution.
Notice the remarkable details given here and check each
one of them against Matthew 27:26-30. Yet all of these

formed part of a vast body of prophecy extending right
back through the Old Testament, all of which was to be
fulfilled to the letter (v.31). The disciples were still
baffled by it all (v.34), but for us, who know that they
were fulfilled, these prophecies should help us to grasp
the amazing authority and accuracy of the whole Bible.

The faith he rewarded
The story of the healing of the blind man is vividly and
dramatically told (vv.35-43). Perhaps the most out-
standing thing to notice is the blind man's faith. Whereas
the crowd explained the commotion to him by saying
that 'Jesus of Nazareth is passing by' (v.37), he cried out
to him as 'Jesus, Son of David' (v.38) — a title reserved
exclusively for the Messiah (see Jeremiah 23:5). The
blind man may not have realized all that this meant, but
he fervently pinned his faith in the one whom he believed
to be the Christ. God's promise is that that kind of faith
will never go unrewarded (2 Chronicles 20:20) and for
the blind man it brought instant healing (v.42), for
which he in turn gave all the glory to God (v.43).

'The God we serve is able to save us' (Daniel 3:17).

49

From Jericho to Jerusalem (1)
Luke 19:1-27

Luke now begins to give us much more detail about the
location of his narrative. The blind man was healed as

Jesus approached Jericho (look back to 18:35); this new
chapter begins with him passing through that city (v.1),
which was about twenty miles from Jerusalem. By verse
29 he had reached Bethany, about eighteen miles on; by
verse 41 he was in sight of Jerusalem and at verse 45 he
entered the city which was to see the climax of his earthly
life. In today's reading, Luke records just one extended
incident, in which a rich man becomes a Christian and
Jesus teaches a very serious lesson about Christian
responsibility.

The man who was converted

Jericho was a popular winter resort, an important
trading centre and world-famous for its balsam groves.
Zacchaeus is introduced as 'a chief tax-collector' (v.2) —
obviously a senior officer in what must have been a
thriving department of the Civil Service in a wealthy
town like Jericho. We are also told that he was rich,
perhaps partly as the result of lining his pockets by fraud.
Hearing that Jesus was in town, he was determined to
see him, perhaps because he had heard that this
remarkable preacher actually welcomed tax-collectors,
whereas most people hated them like poison (see 15:1,2).
As he was not tall enough to see over people's heads, he
climbed up a sycamore-fig tree (v.4). When Jesus arrived
he called Zacchaeus down and invited himself to his
house (v.5). The crowd muttered their usual disapproval
(v.7), but the effect on Zacchaeus was instant and
astonishing. In a moment of time he became 'a new
creation' (2 Corinthians 5:17). He obeyed Jesus immediately and welcomed him to his house (v.6). What is
more, he announced his intention of giving half his
possessions to charity and of repaying all the people he
had swindled, with 300% interest (v.8), whereas even in
a case of proven fraud the law only required the addition
of 20% to the capital sum involved! (See Numbers
5:5-7.) No wonder Jesus was able to be so definite about

Zacchaeus' conversion (v.9), declaring him a true, spiritual son of Abraham! (See Galatians 3:6,7.) Jesus added that it was precisely to carry out this kind of life-saving mission that he had come into the world (compare v.10 with 1 Timothy 1:15).

The men who were commended

While the people were still listening, Jesus went on to tell them a parable, this time to correct the thinking of those who still hoped that he was about to set up an earthly kindom at Jerusalem (v.11). As with all parables, we are not meant to squeeze a detailed meaning out of every word, but rather to grasp the general picture and the main lessons. In this case, the main meaning comes across if we see the 'man of noble birth' as representing Jesus and the 'ten servants' as representing all Christians. In a nutshell, Jesus was teaching that though he would indeed be 'appointed king' (link v.12 with Revelation 17:14) he must first go into 'a distant country' (v.12), that is, heaven (see John 14:1,2). In the meantime, his servants had work to do in hostile surroundings (vv.13,14). When the nobleman returned, the servants who had been diligent were rewarded (vv.15-19), the one who had done nothing useful was impoverished (vv.20-24) and his rebellious enemies were destroyed (v.27). Christ has entrusted us with the stewardship of every gift we have, including the gospel itself (see 1 Thessalonians 2:4) and we are answerable to him for all we do (look up 2 Corinthians 5:10). Whether or not we receive the kind of reward mentioned in the parable will depend entirely on the quality of our stewardship (see 1 Corinthians 3:11-15).

'May our Lord Jesus Christ himself and God our Father. . . encourage your hearts and strengthen you in every good deed and word' (2 Thessalonians 2:16,17).

50

From Jericho to Jerusalem (2)
Luke 19:28-46

After the story of Zacchaeus' conversion, Luke tells us
nothing else about Jesus' journey towards Jerusalem
until he reaches Bethany, almost on the outskirts of the
city. Here, Jesus seems to have put a pre-arranged plan
into operation. He told two disciples to go ahead to
the next village and bring back a young donkey they
would find there (compare v.30 with Matthew 21:2).
If questioned, they were to give what sounds like a kind
of password: 'The Lord needs it' (v.31). Exactly as
arranged, the donkey was brought (vv.32-35) and Jesus
began the final two-mile journey into Jerusalem. Luke's
narrative focuses attention on three events that took
place.

The praise that was offered
The annual Feast of the Passover was now approaching
and for Jesus to enter Jerusalem at a time when the
authorities would be particularly alert showed great
courage. There was an undisguised determination to kill
him and people doubted whether he would risk attending
the feast at all (see John 11:53-57). But Jesus knew that
this was his God-ordained pathway and he was determined to follow it (see 9:51). Not only did he enter the
city openly, but his choice of transport was vividly
significant. An Old Testament prophet had made it clear

the Messiah would enter Jerusalem riding on a young
donkey (see Zechariah 9:9) and here was Jesus fulfilling
that prophecy to the letter. When they put all of this
alongside the many miracles they had seen him perform
(v.37), the crowds went wild with delight, even shouting
words from a messianic psalm to express their feelings
(link v.38 with Psalm 118:26). When some of the
Pharisees told him to put a stop to all of this, Jesus told
them that nothing could hold back the acclamation
which was rightly due to him (vv.39,40). Although he
knew that much of it was superficial, Jesus accepted his
worship by the people as his divine right (see Philippians
2:9-11).

The pain that was felt
But in the middle of this triumphant day Jesus suddenly
broke down in tears (v.41). The cause of his sorrow was
because he knew what would follow Jerusalem's spiritual
blindness and her failure to respond to his message (v.42
and the end of v.44). The prophecy he made (vv.43,44)
was literally fulfilled in A.D.70 when Jerusalem was first
besieged and then destroyed by Roman armies, resulting
in a terrible massacre that could have been avoided had
the Jews followed his peaceful pathways rather than their
own hot-headed ideas (link v.42 with 1:79). But there is a
wider fulfilment of this prophecy which the Bible applies
to all those who reject the reign of Christ and his gracious
gospel invitation. Paul spells it out in the solemn words
of 2 Thessalonians 1:7-9.

The purging that was needed
Soon after his arrival in the city (Mark tells us that it was
on the following day, see Mark 11:11-15) Jesus went into
the temple area and drove out the traders selling
sacrificial animals (v.45) and overturned the tables of the
money-changers (see Mark 11:15). Under the Jewish
religious system both facilities would have been very

helpful, but many of the operators were notoriously
dishonest and that kind of thing going on within the
temple precincts drove Jesus to take drastic action. It is
surprising not to read of a violent reaction by the
authorities, but perhaps the reason is that Jesus was able
to enlist their cherished Old Testament prophets in
defence of his action (compare v.46 with Isaiah 56:7 and
Jeremiah 7:11). Do you have a genuine concern for the
glory of God and courage in facing opposition and
countering evil in today's society?

'The Lord abhors dishonest scales' (Proverbs 11:1).

51

Questions and answers (1)

Luke 19:47-20:19

Jesus had now entered the last week of his earthly life
and the scene was being set for its dramatic climax. He
was in Jerusalem, the very headquarters of enemies bent
on his destruction (19:47). Yet he went fearlessly on,
going openly to the temple area every day, 'teaching the
people. . . and preaching the gospel' (20:1). These days
are covered by Luke in the next two chapters (look ahead
to 21:37,38). Much more must have been said than has
been recorded, but we can learn important lessons from
the teaching preserved for us here, much of it sparked off
by questions put to Jesus.

The authority of Jesus

The first question came from 'the chief priests and the
teachers of the law' (v.1) — the religious experts — and
we can understand why they put their double-barrelled
challenge (v.2). After all, Jesus had swept into the temple
area, disrupting things left, right and centre. Who did he
think he was? Notice, incidentally, that they had sent a
team to investigate John the Baptist in a similar way
when he burst on the scene a few years earlier (John
1:19-22). Rather than give a direct reply, Jesus asked a
question about John's ministry (vv.3,4). Now they were
cornered! While they had rejected John, he had been
very popular with the people (see Matthew 3:5). More
importantly, John had clearly said that he was preparing
the way for Jesus, whom he called 'the Son of God' (see
John 1:29-34). Now if they acknowledged that John was
a genuine prophet sent from God, they would be
condemned for rejecting him and for rejecting his
testimony about Jesus (v.5); on the other hand, they
were afraid to disown John in case of a violent reaction
by the crowd (v.6); compare Herod's dilemma in
Matthew 14:5. In the end, they pretended that they were
incapable of coming to a decision on the matter (v.7).
Jesus refused to trade words with such hypocritical liars
(v.8). He was under no obligation to answer dishonest
questions.

Jesus and the authorities

Jesus now turned to the crowd (v.9) and told them a
parable which both answered the original question and
condemned those who rejected it. The story itself is
simple enough (vv.9-16), but the obvious interpretation
infuriated the religious leaders (v.19). They would have
remembered the same kind of picture used by one of the
great Old Testament prophets (Isaiah 5:1-7) and they
would have no difficulty in identifying the items and
people in the parable. The 'man' was God; the 'vineyard'

was Israel; they themselves and their predecessors were
the 'tenants'; the 'servants' were the prophets and the
'son' was Jesus. Everything fitted perfectly! When the
people thought through the point about the vineyard
being given to 'others' — which could only mean the
inclusion of Gentiles in the kingdom of God — they were
aghast (v.16). Jesus now drove home the point about his
authority by quoting from the very psalm the crowd had
used in welcoming him into the city (link v.17 with
Psalm 118:22). Peter applied the same quotation to Jesus
more than once (Acts 4:11; 1 Peter 2:7,8) and of course
the issue is crucial. Notice how solemnly Jesus put this in
verse 18. If a person strikes himself against Christ in
opposition or unbelief he will do himself irreparable
harm (compare Isaiah 45:9) and if the day comes when
Christ falls on him in judgement, he will be utterly
destroyed.

All of this is a reminder to us of the solemn issues
involved in seeking to witness for Christ. People's
reaction to the gospel is not just a matter of opinion; it is
a matter of life or death. What is your reaction to 2
Corinthians 2:16,17?

'God has made. . . Jesus. . . both Lord and Christ' (Acts 2:36).

———————————— **52** ————————————

Questions and answers (2)

Luke 20:20-40

By now the enemies of Jesus were watching him like
hawks, looking for an opportunity to have him killed (see
19:47). But with amazing courage, Jesus continued to
teach quite openly. Today's reading contains two
questions and the answers Jesus gave to them.

The matter of taxation

As their direct attacks had failed, the enemies of Jesus
now sent spies into the front line (v.20). These were not
themselves teachers of the law or Pharisees, but some of
their students (compare Matthew 22:16). They began
with a hefty dose of flattery (v.21). Neither they nor their
masters believed a word of this. It was just a crude device
to give the impression of being honest men who
recognized truth when they heard it. Then came their
carefully worded question (v.22). No doubt infuriated
that Jesus had placed them in a quandary (v.4), they felt
that this would put him in an even worse dilemma. The
tax concerned was levied by the Romans; it amounted to
just a few pence a year, but had to be paid in Roman
currency. The coin used was the silver denarius, which
bore the head of the emperor and words which virtually
described him as a divine ruler. It therefore caused great
offence to the Jews (see Acts 5:36,37). The dilemma was

this: if Jesus said it was wrong to pay tax he would be
arrested by the Romans; if he said it was right, he would
offend his Jewish followers. But Jesus saw straight
through the trick. He took a denarius and asked, 'Whose
portrait and inscription are on it?' (v.24) When they
replied 'Caesar's' he laid down a masterly principle
(v.25). To use Caesar's coins was to acknowledge his
authority and to accept an obligation to pay what was
legally due to him. We have a duty to pay for the
privileges our government and society provide (see
Romans 13:1-7). But where the law of man and the
law of God conflict, our duty is equally clear (see Acts
5:27-29). God has the greater kingdom and the prior
claim (see Daniel 4:34). In the face of such precise yet
perfect wisdom, the spies were silenced (v.26).

The matter of resurrection

The Sadducees were a sect who did not believe in angels,
spirits or resurrection (compare v.27 with Acts 23:8).
They also treated the books of Moses (Genesis-
Deuteronomy) as superior to the rest of the Old
Testament. They now came to Jesus, quoted Moses (link
v.28 with Deuteronomy 25:5,6), recited an unlikely story
(vv.29-32) and asked a question (v.33). They probably
argued that as this would produce a ridiculous situation,
the whole idea of resurrection could be dismissed. In
reply, Jesus said two basic things. Firstly, even their
great hero, Moses, had implied that the dead rise again,
as he had spoken of the God of Abraham, Isaac and
Jacob (link v.37 with Exodus 3:6). Surely God was the
God of these men as living beings and not just as piles of
bones? (v.38) Secondly, in their resurrected state, people
are 'like the angels' in that 'they can no longer die'
(v.36). As there is no death in heaven, there is no
need for birth and therefore no need for marriage.
The Sadducees' question was therefore a monumental
irrelevance. Matthew 22:29 exposes it in another way!

The Bible does not give us a detailed description of life in heaven and we dare not try to fill in the gaps. Yet what we *are* told is surely enough to make Christians long for that day when in the fullest sense they shall know the experience of being 'God's children' (v.36; compare 1 John 3:2).

Yet the Christian's hope is meant to be more than 'pie in the sky when we die'. It should be a powerful incentive to godly living here and now. Are *you* conscious that your hope of heaven affects your life on earth?

'[The body] is sown in dishonour, it is raised in glory' (1 Corinthians 15:43).

53

Questions and answers (3)

Luke 20:41-21:4

Today's reading is our third in Luke's coverage of the teaching Jesus gave in Jerusalem during the week leading up to his death. This passage covers three distinct and unrelated sections.

A lesson about prophecy

The answer Jesus had given to the Sadducees about the doctrine of resurrection had put paid to any further questions (see v.40). The teachers of the law took some satisfaction from this particular exchange, for there was little love lost between them and the Sadducees. But they had hardly finished congratulating Jesus on his victory (v.39) before he challenged them with questions of his own. Matthew tells us that he first asked whose son (that is, descendant) they thought the Christ (the Messiah) was (see Matthew 22:42). They had no problem in answering that he was 'David's'. The Old Testament stated it (see 2 Samuel 7:12,13) and they themselves taught it (see John 7:42, for instance). That explains the question Luke records (vv.41,44). In between the questions, Jesus quoted the opening verse of Psalm 110 (vv.42,43) and said that David was speaking about the Messiah (compare Acts 2:34,35; 1 Corinthians 15:25). But David had referred to the Messiah not as 'my Son' but as 'my Lord'. Jesus' second question therefore meant, 'How then can Messiah merely be David's physical descendant?' Nobody could answer that (see Matthew 22:46) and Jesus left it there. For the moment, he wanted to make just one point clear: Christ was not only David's descendant, he was his Lord and God; not just his successor, but his Sovereign. He would add the final truth later (see Matthew 26:63,64; compare Romans 1:3). When it comes to the person of Jesus, there is no identity crisis in the Bible!

A lesson about hypocrisy

Throughout his ministry, Jesus reserved some of his most withering attacks for the sin of hypocrisy. He now singled out the scribes for particular attention. They loved to project themselves as being both pious and important (v.46). But even their long-winded prayers were insincere and just 'for a show' (v.47). Underneath, they were self-centred and greedy and would even wheedle extravagant personal gifts out of helpless widows in the name of religion. Jesus bluntly promised that such men 'will be punished most severely' (v.47). The person who reads these words should examine his actions and motives with very great care!

A lesson about generosity

Part of the temple area was the Court of the Women, which contained thirteen collecting-boxes shaped like upturned trumpets. It was into one of these boxes that Jesus saw certain rich people placing their gifts (21:1). He then saw a very poor widow put in 'two very small copper coins' (v.2). This particular coin (also mentioned at 12:59) was the *lepton*, the smallest Jewish coin of all. Yet Jesus said that this widow put in 'more than all the others' (v.3). Why? Because the others had given a token of their plenty, whereas she had given the total of her poverty (v.4). Few things test a Christian's spirituality better than the way he uses money. The Bible teaches us that we are to give willingly (1 Chronicles 29:9), proportionately (Deuteronomy 16:17), generously (Matthew 10:8) and worshipfully (Proverbs 3:9). Check these principles through very carefully. Few things are a better index of a person's spirituality than their attitude towards their material possessions. Are you as careful about your standard of giving as your standard of living?

'A generous man will himself be blessed' (Proverbs 22:9).

54

Troubles and triumph to come (1)

Luke 21:5-19

The setting for the main part of this remarkable chapter comes at the very end, where Luke tells us the daily routine Jesus followed (look ahead to vv.37,38). As Jesus was leaving the temple one afternoon, some of the disciples commented on its great beauty (v.5). To their amazement, Jesus said that the day was coming when it would be razed to the ground (v.6). When they reached the Mount of Olives, four of them asked him when this would happen and what the warning signs would be (v.7, read Mark 13:1-4 for details omitted by Luke). These two questions led Jesus into a remarkable series of prophecies relating to the destruction of Jerusalem, the end of the world and his own personal return to the earth. Most of the chapter is taken up with signs and warnings, but there are also words of encouragement and the promise of the ultimate triumph of God and his people. Today's reading is generally concerned with the fall of Jerusalem and Jesus outlines three ways in which, before that happens, the Christians' faith will be tested.

Deception

In a previous prophecy about the end of the world, Jesus had warned his disciples about people who would make supernatural claims (look back to 17:20-23); now he underlined the same thing (v.8). There is an example of this kind of thing happening in Acts 8:9,10. The disciples' instructions in this kind of situation were crystal clear: 'Do not follow them' (v.8). Some religious and philosophical leaders make similar claims today; Christians' instructions have not changed!

Disruption

Jesus next prophesied that there would be a breakdown in international relationships (v.10), something later recorded by reliable historians. Then there would be disruption both on the earth and in the sky (v.11). The historian Josephus records one of these 'great signs from heaven' (v.11) — a comet in the shape of a sword which hung pointed over Jerusalem for a whole year. Signs like these must have terrified many people; it was typically gracious of Jesus to prepare his people for them, so that they need be neither surprised nor terrified.

Detestation

But there was more personal trouble ahead for the Christians and Jesus now told them what that would be. Because of their faith, they would be persecuted and put on trial by both Jews — they would deliver them to synagogues — and Gentiles — 'kings and governors' (v.12). Worse still, some would be betrayed by members of their own families (v.16). The seeds of this warning had been sown earlier (see 12:52,53) now the full truth must be told. Yet out of all of this hatred, bitterness and cruelty, a great deal of good would come. Firstly, their arrest and trial would give Christians an opportunity to bear witness for Christ (v.13; notice also what Paul said in Philippians 1:12-14). Secondly, in these moments of crisis Jesus promised that he would give them 'words and wisdom that none of your adversaries will be able to resist or contradict' (v.15). Compare this with what Jesus had said earlier (12:11,12) and notice how exactly this promise was fulfilled in the case of Stephen (Acts 6:10). Thirdly, although some of them would be put to death (v.16) none of them would come to any harm! (v.18) As we saw earlier, even the power of a godless executioner is strictly limited! (12:4) As God's children, they were eternally secure in his loving hands and they would gain everything by 'standing firm' (v.19). These promises must have been a tremendous comfort to those first disciples. The principles they contain are no less precious to those who faithfully seek to follow Christ today.

'The angel of the Lord encamps around those who fear him, and he delivers them' (Psalm 34:7).

55

Troubles and triumph
to come (2)

Luke 21:20-38

Today's reading continues the remarkable series of
prophecies, warnings and instructions which Jesus gave
in answer to the disciples' original questions about the
forthcoming destruction of Jerusalem (v.7). In this
closing section, Jesus specifically deals with the fall of the
city, but then widens his comments to include events to
take place at his second coming and the end of the world.

The terrible ruin of Jerusalem

The final sign that the city's destruction was near would
be that hostile troops would begin to surround it (link
v.20 with 19:43). From then on, the city's doom was
inevitable, both as a punishment and as a fulfilment of
prophecy (link v.22 with 19:44). There would therefore
be no point in heroic resistance. The Christians should
get out — quickly! (v.21) The historian Eusebius says
that the Christians in the city when the siege began
(A.D.70) did exactly as they had been instructed and
escaped across the River Jordan to the city of Pella. It
was as well that they did, because the terrible savagery
which Jesus prophesied in verses 23 and 24 then fell on
the doomed city. One historian speaks of over 1,000,000
people killed and 97,000 young men taken into captivity;
not one Jew was left alive in the whole city! From then
on, Jerusalem was 'trampled on by the Gentiles' (v.24)

for one century after another. The phrase 'until the times
of the Gentiles are fulfilled' may mean something like
'until the Gentiles have had all of the full opportunity
God intends them to have to respond to the gospel'.
Speculation as to when that might be is both foolish and
futile.

The triumphant return of Jesus

From verse 25 onwards, Jesus seems to be referring to the
events surrounding his second coming (notice vv.27,36).
As with the fall of Jerusalem, Christ's return will be
preceded by spectacular and fearful happenings. Compare verses 25-36 with verses 10,11 and notice that both
sections include upheavals on the earth and extraordinary phenomena in the sky. Notice, too, what is said in 2
Peter 3:10-12. Not surprisingly, Jesus said that men
would 'faint from terror, apprehensive of what is coming
on the world' (v.26), but Christians are to 'stand up' and
lift up their heads (v.28). Their confidence is to be based
on the kind of certainty illustrated by Jesus in a tiny
parable (vv.29,30). These terrible events would mean
that two things, both closely connected, were very near
— the kingdom of God and the Christians' full and final
redemption (vv.31,28). Notice how Paul uses the same
comforting truth that for Christians living on earth
salvation is something in the future, but drawing nearer
all the time (Romans 13:11). Jesus next went on to say
that, however appalling their persecution, the Jewish
race would survive until the end of time (this is the
probable meaning of v.32). All of these things were
guaranteed by the fact that Christ's words were indes-
tructible (v.33), as is all of God's Word (look back to
16:17 and compare Isaiah 40:8; 1 Peter 1:24,25). Having
given such a full and loving warning, Jesus went on to
say that the actual day of his return would come as
suddenly as a trap being sprung (v.34 and look back to
17:24 for another illustration Jesus used to say the same

thing). That being so, Christians should be 'always on
the watch' (v.36). In particular, they should avoid
'dissipation, drunkenness and the anxieties of life' (v.34).
Selfish indulgence in pleasure or self-centred preoccupation with work is poor preparation for the Lord's
return. If these warnings were true when they were first
spoken, they are nearly 2,000 years more urgently true
today!

'Everyone who has this hope in him purifies himself' (1 John
3:3).

56

The Last Supper (1)

Luke 22:1-23

With the end of the last chapter, Luke came to the close
of his account of Christ's public ministry. Now he moves
on to the events surrounding his death. In the opening
part of this chapter, three key things are mentioned, the
last two blending together in a remarkable way.

A record of Judas' defection
Judas Iscariot is one of the most tragic figures in the
whole Bible. Called to be a follower of Jesus (see
Matthew 10:4) he moved so intimately in the disciples'
circle that he became the group's treasurer (see John
13:29). But he misused his office and swindled the others
by stealing money from the funds (see John 12:6). Now
he did something infinitely worse: he went to the

authorities and suggested that he should betray Jesus
(v.4). We are not told why he did such an appalling
thing, but perhaps he was disgusted that he was not,
after all, going to share in the glory of an earthly
kingdom set up by Jesus. Needless to say, money was
involved (v.5) and we are told elsewhere that the price
agreed was 'thirty silver coins' (see Matthew 26:14,15).
Shamefully, this was the amount of compensation a man
would have to pay if his ox gored another man's slave
(see Exodus 21:32); amazingly, it was the exact amount
prophesied over 500 years earlier! (Look up Zechariah
11:12,13.) Judas managed to cover up his plot very
skilfully (vv.21-23), but he would eventually have to pay
a terrible price (v.22). Judas stands as a terrible warning
that neither mixing with other Christians nor holding
office in the church is any guarantee of a man's salvation.
Although he was often *at* Christ's side, Judas was never
really *on* Christ's side (see John 13:10,11) and the devil
was able to use him at will (link v.3 with John 6:70).

A reminder of the Jews' deliverance

The Jewish Feast of Unleavened Bread was loosely
called the Passover (v.1) though in fact they were two
separate events celebrated at the same time. The
Passover commemorated the deliverance of the Jews
after 430 years' captivity in Egypt (see Exodus 12,
especially vv.14,24-27,40-42). The Feast of Unleavened
Bread was another simple yet vivid reminder of the same
marvellous event in their history (see Exodus 12:15-20;
13:3-10). No faithful Jew would fail to carry out these
clear instructions. Continual gratitude for all the
Lord's goodness is a sure mark of spirituality (see 1
Thessalonians 5:18); forgetfulness of his kindness is
always a dangerous sign (see Jeremiah 3:21).

A representation of Jesus' death

As they reclined at table, Jesus told the disciples how

much he had looked forward to this special meal (v.15), but that this would be the last Passover he would celebrate with them on earth (vv.16,18). During a normal Passover meal, those taking part would share three cakes of unleavened bread and drink from four cups of wine. Jesus now took these familiar things and used them as symbols of his forthcoming death (vv.19,20). In particular he said that his death would establish a new covenant for his people (as prophesied at Jeremiah 31:31-34). Then, in the simplest possible way, he instructed his disciples to continue this lovely ceremony as a permanent reminder of his death on their behalf (link vv.19,20 with 1 Corinthians 11:23-26). We cannot be sure how much of this the disciples fully understood at the time, but within a few years the Lord's Supper, as it became known, had replaced the Passover ceremony as far as Christians were concerned. Ever since, it has been a sacred and solemn reminder of our Saviour's death (see 1 Corinthians 10:16,17) and its observance part of the Christian's obedience.

'Christ, our Passover lamb, has been sacrificed. Therefore let us keep the Festival' (1 Corinthians 5:7,8).

57

The Last Supper (2)

Luke 22:24-38

In today's reading, Luke continues his account of the last Passover meal Jesus had with his disciples, a meal which he turned into the first Lord's Supper (or Holy Communion), the symbol of the new covenant which he was shortly to establish with his own blood (see Hebrews 13:20). The pieces of conversation which Luke records, focusing on the teaching Jesus gave, can be grouped into three paragraphs.

The pride he condemned

It seems terrible that with Jesus speaking so movingly about his death (now only a few hours away) the disciples should still be arguing about which of them should be 'considered to be the greatest' (v.24). They had done this kind of thing before (see Mark 9:33-35), but they had obviously not learned the lesson Jesus taught them on that occasion. Jesus now condemned their attitude as downright worldly — the kind of thing godless kings did. Some Syrian and Egyptian kings actually took the title of 'Benefactor' to draw attention to their authority; this explains the reference in verse 25. Jesus then went on to say that Christian behaviour should be exactly the opposite (v.26). The love of titles, prestige and authority are wrong in the world and worse in the church and Christians with gifts which make them candidates for leadership should examine their motives with particular and honest care (link Jeremiah 45:5 with 1 Peter 5:2,3). As Jesus had pointed out earlier, there are inflexible laws governing this whole area (check Mark 9:35 again). What is more, he himself was the perfect illustration of the principles he laid down. In Old Testament prophecy he was described as a 'servant' (Isaiah 42:1); speaking of his own life he said that 'The Son of Man did not come to be served, but to serve' (Mark 10:45); John tells us that at the Last Supper Jesus actually washed the disciples' feet (John 13:3,4) and Paul puts into one stupendous statement the Saviour's greatest act of humility and his greatest honour as a result! (Philippians 2:5-11.)

The privilege he conferred

Jesus next went on to tell the disciples that as those who had been faithful to him, they were all to be given a kingdom (v.29), in the sense that they would share in the honour and joy of his own eternal reign (v.30). The phrase 'judging the twelve tribes of Israel' may be a symbolic way of expressing this. The disciples were squabbling over who should be chairman, while Jesus was promising them that they would be kings! Check your own earthly ambitions in the light of 1 Peter 1:3-5.

The pressure he considered

But all of this was in the future. Before that, there were pressures to face and Jesus now considered these. He told Peter that Satan had asked God for permission to test the disciples very seriously (compare v.31 with Job 1:6-12; 2:1-7). The inference then seems to be that the disciples would crack under pressure, but that Peter, although he, too, would waver badly, would help them to recover their faith (vv.32-34). Incidentally, notice how these verses indicate Christ's deity; no mere man could possibly have known all these things. Finally, Jesus then warned them to prepare for the next, more difficult phase of their lives. Thus far, there had been special provision for their brief bursts of evangelistic activity (v.35); from now on, they would need to make sensible provision for their maintenance and defence (v.36). Misunderstanding his reference to buying swords, they told Jesus that they had two already (v.38). In reply Jesus said, 'That is enough' (v.38), obviously not meaning that two would be sufficient to defend eleven men against all their enemies, but rather that they should stop using such aggressive and militant language. The kingdom of God is not won by a military campaign.

'The weapons we fight with are not the weapons of the world' (2 Corinthians 10:4).

58

Despised and rejected

Luke 22:39-71

About 700 years before he came to earth, it was
prophesied of Jesus that he would be 'despised and
rejected by men, a man of sorrows, and familiar with
suffering' (Isaiah 53:3). The terrible truth of all that this
means now begins to unfold.

Agony
When the Last Supper was over, Jesus went with the
disciples to the Mount of Olives (v.39). Here, he left the
disciples for a while to pray alone (v.41). His prayer was
simple, yet tremendously profound, and we are on holy
ground in trying to grasp its full meaning (v.42). Because
he was truly human he naturally shrank from the terrible
death which faced him the next morning, so he prayed
that God should deliver him from it, 'If you are willing'
(v.42). Yet because his will was totally submitted to the
will of God, he added, 'Yet not my will, but yours be
done' (v.42). Here is a model prayer, showing that God
constantly requires our submission to his sovereignty
(compare Matthew 6:10). Even with the comfort of an
angel (v.43), the agony of the experience was so great for
Jesus that blood oozed from his pores and mingled with
the sweat that dripped from his face.

Treachery

Meantime, the disciples had been asleep, 'exhausted from sorrow' (v.45). Later, as Jesus was talking to them, Judas appeared with a mob armed with swords and clubs (link v.47 with Matthew 26:47). To prevent a wrongful arrest, Judas had arranged to identify Jesus with a kiss (link the end of v.47 with Matthew 26:48). The disciples were all for fighting it out (v.49) and one of them — John tells us it was Peter (see John 18:10) — had actually slashed a man's ear off before being told, 'No more of this!' (vv.50,51; compare this with v.38). Turning to the crowd, Jesus inferred that even the timing of his arrest was God-ordained (vv.52,53).

Tragedy

Jesus was taken straight to the house of the high priest, Peter following 'at a distance' (v.54). The other disciples had run away (see Mark 14:50) and Peter's personal tragedy was soon to follow. While Jesus was on trial for his life, Peter was on trial for his loyalty (vv.55-59). Though he was positively identified and his accent proved he was a Galilean (v.59), he flatly denied that he knew Jesus at all. Just as he lied for the third time, the cock crowed (v.60). One look from Jesus was enough to remind Peter of what he had said a few hours earlier (link v.61 with 22:34). Peter 'went outside and wept bitterly' (v.62), but they were tears of repentance and they marked the beginning of the way back. It is the man with no tears for his sin who is to be pitied.

Mockery

When this first trial was over, Jesus was left in the custody of the guards, who mocked him, beat him, spat in his face (link v.63 with Matthew 26:67) and even played a crude game of Blind Man's Buff with him (v.64). Yet even this mockery was a fulfilment of prophecy (see Isaiah 50:6).

'Blasphemy'

The examination before the high priest was not strictly
legal, as no trial on a charge carrying the death penalty
was allowed at night. So at the crack of dawn, the council
(or Sanhedrin) was hurriedly assembled. When they
asked Jesus if he was the Christ (the Messiah) he told
them that their question was insincere (vv.67,68), then
added a statement that prompted an even more dramatic
question (vv.69,70). To that, Jesus replied, 'You are
right in saying I am' (v.70). That made it an open and
shut case as far as the council was concerned. This was
downright blasphemy (compare 5:21) for which there
was only one penalty (link v.71 with Matthew 26:65,66).
But Jesus was not prepared to save his life at the expense
of the truth.

'This is my Son, whom I love; with him I am well pleased'
(Matthew 3:17).

59

Count-down to Calvary

Luke 23:1-25

The trial by the Sanhedrin had been a farce because the
members had decided on their verdict before the trial
began! (Read John 11:47-53.) But they were still not able
to carry out the death penalty (see John 18:31). That
power lay with the Romans, who would not be interested
in Jewish religious law. Some kind of political charge was
needed. Luke now continues his story.

Malevolence

Thirsting for blood, 'The whole assembly rose and led [Jesus] off to Pilate' (v.1). The three new charges they laid against him (note these in v.2) were all maliciously untrue. (For example, contrast the second charge with 20:25!) Taken together, they accused Jesus of being a political agitator. From Pilate's examination of Jesus, Luke records only one question (v.3). The reply he received obviously satisfied Pilate that Jesus was no threat whatever to Roman security and he passed a verdict of 'Not Guilty' (v.4). The council was furious and insisted that Jesus had caused trouble all the way from Galilee. The mention of Galilee gave Pilate an idea, because it came under the control of Herod Antipas, who was then in Jerusalem. Pilate jumped at the chance to evade any further responsibility and by showing that he recognized Herod's jurisdiction he would help to patch up a quarrel that existed between them (vv.6,7,12). But was this yet another fulfilment of prophecy? Look at Psalm 2:2,3.

Silence

Herod was delighted. It would be great fun to have a close look at this fellow, especially if he turned on a miracle or two (link v.8 with 9:9). But in one of the most dreadful phrases in the Bible we read that Jesus 'gave him no answer' (v.9). What a solemn warning to those who treat God in a casual or trivial way! Nothing is more terrible than God's silence. Frustrated and angry, Herod responded by joining the soldiers in poking fun at Jesus before sending him back to Pilate (v.11).

Innocence

Pilate began by reminding everyone that neither he nor Herod could find Jesus guilty of any capital offence (vv.13-15). Clearly wanting to let him go, he suggested a compromise. Perhaps a good beating would teach Jesus a

lesson and he could then be released (v.16). The release
could take place under special arrangement (see v.17
which seems to have been inserted from Mark 15:6).
This prisoner was chosen by popular demand and Pilate
offered the crowd two candidates — Jesus and Barabbas,
a murderous rebel (compare vv.18,19 with Matthew
27:15-17). When the crowd asked for the release of
Barabbas, Pilate 'appealed to them again' (v.20), but
this only seemed to make things worse, for the crowd
now started screaming for Jesus to be crucified (v.21).
Pilate made one final appeal, again offering to beat Jesus
before releasing him (v.22), but by now the mob was in
full cry. One man had nothing to say (see 1 Peter 2:23).

Sentence

Luke's report of the sentence is concise and chilling:
Pilate simply gave in to the mob (v.25). Yet neither
Pilate nor the mob was in control. Jesus himself had
already made it clear that be would be mocked,
scourged and crucified (see Matthew 20:17-19). Little
did Pilate and the mob know that as Jesus was led away,
it was their hands that were tied, not his! This passage
brings us to the very brink of man's greatest ever crime
and the darkest hour in history, but we must never read
of them without realizing that throughout it all God was
neither surprised nor defeated.

*'This man was handed over. . . by God's set purpose and
foreknowledge'* (Acts 2:23).

60

Last words

Luke 23:26-56

We come now to the climax of all that has gone before — the death of Jesus. In today's study we shall simply concentrate on the last words of Jesus recorded by Luke (Matthew, Mark and John mention others).

The word of sorrow
As Jesus began the journey to the place of execution, a great crowd followed, including women from Jerusalem who 'mourned and wailed for him' (v.27), sensing, perhaps, that quite apart from anything else, there had been a terrible miscarriage of justice. In a moment of superb selflessness, Jesus turned and said that they should be weeping for themselves and for their children (v.28). He was obviously thinking of the coming destruction of Jerusalem, when it would be better to be childless than to see one's children slaughtered (v.29). On that day, people would want the earth to swallow them up (link v.30 with Hosea 10:8). Verse 31 is a proverb which probably meant: 'If they do this to someone who is innocent, what will they do to the guilty, that is, the Jews?' Notice what is said in 1 Peter 4:17,18.

The word of sympathy
Jesus had already told his followers to love their enemies and pray for their persecutors (see Matthew 5:43,44).

Now, he proved that this was no empty idealism, for as
he hung on the cross, naked and bleeding, he prayed,
'Father, forgive them, for they do not know what they are
doing' (v.34). The Romans certainly had no idea they
were fulfilling prophecy! (Link vv.33,34 with Psalm
22:16,18.)

The word of salvation

Two common criminals were being executed at the same
time as Jesus (v.32) and they now began cursing him (see
Matthew 27:44). One of them kept on arguing that if he
was the Christ he ought to save all three of them, but a
remarkable change came over the other man. Suddenly,
he rebuked his fellow criminal for insulting Jesus,
admitted his own sin, acknowledged that Jesus was
innocent and the ruler of a spiritual kingdom beyond the
grave, and cried to him for mercy! (vv.40-42) His
repentance and faith were clearly genuine, because Jesus
promised that he would be in heaven with him that very
day (v.43). This beautiful word of salvation is a
marvellous illustration of Romans 10:13 and should be a
great encouragement to us never to write anyone off as
being beyond the reach of God's grace.

The word of surrender

The very last words of Jesus on the cross recorded by
Luke are gentle, simple, but remarkable: 'Father, into
your hands I commit my spirit' (v.46). With his faculties
crystal clear he placed his spirit into his Father's hands
and laid down his life. Check how perfectly this agrees
with John 10:17,18! Jesus is the only man in history who
chose to die. His unique death was marked in several
extraordinary ways (vv.44,45; and see others at Matthew
27:50-53). The 'curtain of the temple' separated the
people from the symbolic presence of God in the Holy of
Holies. This could only mean one thing. Read Hebrews
10:19-22 carefully and gratefully and always remember

that from God's side everything has been done to enable the Christian believer to approach God's throne of grace at any time. Problems in prayer can never be blamed on God! Luke then describes the impression made on the soldier in charge of the execution squad and on the people in general (vv.47,48). He also briefly records the burial of Jesus (vv.50-54) and tells us that certain women from Galilee made a note of where the body lay so that, when the sabbath was over, they could complete the normal Jewish custom of embalming the dead body (vv.55,56). Of the death and burial of Jesus there could be no possible doubt.

'He. . . became obedient to death — even death on a cross!' (Philippians 2:8).

61

Life After Death

Luke 24:1-32

Nothing has ever fascinated man more deeply than the question of whether there is life after death and no man has ever examined the question properly until he has read the New Testament record of the events which followed the crucifixion of Jesus. Luke's last chapter is a vital part of that record.

The empty tomb
The Jewish day began and ended at sunset, which meant that the sabbath ended on our Saturday evening. It was

therefore very early on the Sunday morning, 'the first
day of the week' that several women — some of them are
mentioned in verse 10 — went to the grave to embalm
the body of Jesus (v.1). They were amazed to find no
body (vv.2,3). As they were thinking this through, they
were startled by 'two men in clothes that gleamed like
lightning' (v.4) who suddenly stood beside them (later
identified as angels, v.23). The women were naturally
terrified but were immediately challenged with a
question that went far beyond their feelings (v.5). Then
came the most dramatic announcement in all history:
'He is not here; he has risen!' (v.6) The angel then
reminded them of what Jesus himself had promised
(compare v.7 with 9:22). The women remembered
perfectly well (v.8), which made their actions that
morning a strange mixture of devotion and doubt. They
had come to anoint the body of one who had said he
would no longer be dead! So much of our sorrow today is
because we fail to trust God's Word. Confused and
embarrassed, the women hurried back to tell the other
disciples, but 'their words seemed to them like nonsense'
(v.11). Just to double-check, Peter immediately ran to
the grave where he found nothing except the strips of
linen in which the body had been wrapped. The women
were right and Peter had some thinking to do! (v.12)

The risen Lord

Several hours later, two of the disciples were walking
from Jerusalem to Emmaus, about seven miles away,
and discussing the events of the previous few days
(vv.13,14). Suddenly, Jesus was alongside them, though
in some mysterious way they were prevented from
recognizing him (vv.15,16). When he asked them what
they had been discussing, they were amazed that he
appeared not to have heard the news (vv.17,18). Asked
to explain, they told him the whole sad story (vv.19-24).
They were sick with sorrow. Still unrecognized, Jesus

told them the real cause of their trouble: they had been
'foolish' and 'slow of heart' in their understanding of the
prophets (v.25), or they would have realized that the
Christ *had* to suffer before entering into the fulness of his
glory (v.26). He then gave what must have been the
greatest Old Testament exposition in history — to a
congregation of two! (v.27) No wonder their hearts
burned within them (v.32). By now they were
approaching Emmaus and Jesus accepted their invitation to stay with them (vv.28-30). They sat down to a
meal together and suddenly, as he broke the bread and
gave thanks, they recognized him, and, just as suddenly,
he disappeared (v.31). But they had *seen him,* and from
then on nothing would ever be the same again! Knowing
facts about Jesus is not enough to save a man, as he
himself once made perfectly clear (see John 5:39,40).
True Christianity demands a living encounter with its
Founder (see 2 Timothy 1:12) and such an experience is
gloriously possible because he is alive today. Nothing is
more important to your Christian growth than cultivat-
ing your personal relationship with the risen Christ.
Constantly seek to ensure that this is your greatest
priority.

*'Jesus our Lord. . . was delivered over to death for our sins and
was raised to life for our justification,* (Romans 4:24,25).

62

The end of the beginning

Luke 24:33-53

Luke's narrative comes to an end in a perfect climax, which we can summarize in four separate paragraphs.

The agreement of the stories

We begin at Emmaus, with two disciples staring at an empty chair in which Jesus had been sitting a moment earlier! Although night was falling (see v.29), they immediately turned back to Jerusalem (v.33) — seven miles along an unlit country road. They found a number of disciples gathered together (v.33) but before the two travellers could get a word in, the others burst out, 'It is true! The Lord has risen and has appeared to Simon' (v.34; see 1 Corinthians 15:5). The two from Emmaus then told their story — down to the last detail! (v.35) Their breathless evidence has since become the testimony of countless millions who have had a life-changing encounter with the living Christ.

The appearance of the Saviour

As they were talking together, Jesus suddenly appeared (v.36). They were terrified at first, thinking that they were seeing a ghost (v.37), perhaps because Jesus had mysteriously got into the room through locked doors (see John 20:19). It is marvellous to notice that Jesus' first concern was to reassure them and replace their fear with faith (vv.38-40). A ghost has neither flesh nor bones and we are clearly told in the Bible that life after death includes the resurrection of the *body* (see Job 19:25,26; 1 Corinthians 15:35-38). Their reaction to this challenge is described perfectly: 'They still did not believe it because of joy and amazement' (v.41). Their emotions swamped their reason! Jesus then asked for some food and ate it in their presence (vv.41-43) — not to meet his needs, but to meet theirs! Peter was to remember this detail vividly (see Acts 10:41).

The attestation of the Scriptures

Jesus then went on to remind them of what he had told them earlier, that *all* the prophecies about him would be fulfilled (v.44). He then made particular mention of his death and resurrection and the universal preaching of the gospel, beginning at Jerusalem (vv.46-48). There is no greater illustration of the Bible's authority than that, at a moment like this, Jesus used it to drive home the great truths which he represented in person. Yet he also wanted to give them an understanding of what he was saying (link v.45 with v.32 and Acts 16:14). Without God's help, nobody can understand God's Word. Psalm 119:18 is an essential prayer when reading the Bible. Then came practical application. The disciples were to preach the gospel as 'witnesses of these things' (v.48). But they would not do this in their own strength; they must first be 'clothed with power from on high' (v.49), a reference to the Holy Spirit (see Acts 1:4,8).

The ascension of the Sovereign

The final scene was at Bethany forty days later (link v.50 with Acts 1:3). Luke's account of the ascension is superbly simple (v.51). For Jesus, it was the perfect climax to all his work on earth; now he went from his crucifixion to his coronation (see Mark 16:19; Acts 2:33; Hebrews 1:3). As for the disciples, their last doubts disappeared. *For the first time* we read that 'They worshipped him' (v.52), a response they could only give to the one to whom they believed all worship was due — the living God. With 'great joy' they went back to Jerusalem to continue their worship (v.53) and eventually to commence their work. For them, as for all Christians, surrender to the claims of Christ marked the end of the beginning!

'Worthy is the Lamb, who was slain, to receive power and wealth and wisdom and strength and honour and glory and praise!' (Revelation 5:12.)